KATUTURA

This series of publications on Africa, Latin America, and Southeast Asia is designed to present significant research, translation, and opinion to area specialists and to a wide community of persons interested in world affairs. The editor seeks manuscripts of quality on any subject and can generally make a decision regarding publication within three months of receipt of the original work. Production methods generally permit a work to appear within one year of acceptance. The editor works closely with authors to produce a high quality book. The series appears in a paperback format and is distributed worldwide. For more information, contact the executive editor at Ohio University Press, Scott Quadrangle, University Terrace, Athens, Ohio 45701.

Executive editor: Gillian Berchowitz
AREA CONSULTANTS
Africa: Diane Ciekawy
Latin America: Thomas Walker
Southeast Asia: James L. Cobban

The Monographs in International Studies series is published for the Center for International Studies by the Ohio University Press. The views expressed in individual monographs are those of the authors and should not be considered to represent the policies or beliefs of the Center for International Studies, the Ohio University Press, or Ohio University.

KATUTURA

A Place Where We Stay

Life in a Post-apartheid
Township in Namibia

Wade C. Pendleton

Ohio University Center for International Studies
Monographs in International Studies
Africa Series, Number 65
Athens

© 1996 by the Center for International Studies, Ohio University
First published 1993 by Gamsberg Macmillan Publishers, Windhoek, Namibia
Printed in the United States of America
02 01 00 99 98 97 96   5 4 3 2 1

The books in the Center for International Studies Monograph Series
are printed on acid-free paper ∞

Library of Congress Cataloging-in-Publication Data

Pendleton, Wade C.
     Katutura : a place where we stay : life in a post-apartheid
township in Namibia / Wade C. Pendleton.
        p.   cm. —(Monographs in international studies. Africa
series ; no. 65)
     Originally published: Windhoek, Namibia : Gamsberg Macmillan,
1993.
     Includes bibliographical references and index.
     ISBN 0-89680-188-8 (pbk.)
     1. Katutura (Windhoek, Namibia) I. Title. II. Series.
DT1680.P46 1996
968.81—dc20   95-51498
                                                    CIP

Cover and text designed by Chiquita Babb
Cover illustration based on a drawing by Joseph Madisia

Acknowledgment of photographs

Julika Komnik: Pages 145, 146, 147, 148
National Archives of Namibia: Pages 63, 64, 65 (bottom), 66, 106 (bottom), 107, 108
Wade C. Pendleton: Pages 65 (top), 106 (top), 109
Jack Cohen: cover photograph of author

"Let Me Tell You This Story" is reproduced with permission
from the poet, Robert Harrison Isaacks

Contents

Tables

Maps, Photographs, and Case Studies

Maps

Photographs

Case Studies

Preface to the 1996 Edition

This edition of *Katutura: A Place Where We Stay* includes a review of literature on urban and African anthropology. In addition, there is also more background information on Namibian towns, communal areas, and commercial farms—for people have migrated to Windhoek and Katutura from all these areas in the past, and continue to do so today. I hope this additional information will enable the reader to better appreciate the context of the book.

My thanks to Robert Gordon for his suggestions concerning additions and revisions for this edition of the book. My appreciation to Mary Bruce Barnes and Michael Whisson for some thoughtful suggestions for revisions. Thanks also to Gillian Berchowitz, Executive Editor of the Ohio University Press Monographs in International Studies for her enthusiasm and support for the publication of this work. My thanks and special appreciation to Debie who continues to help, encourage, support, and share the experiences.

W.C.P.

Harare, Zimbabwe

Preface to the First Edition and Acknowledgments

I did not visit Namibia between 1975 and 1986. I was denied a visa by the South African government and my book *Katutura: A Place Where We Do Not Stay* was submitted to the South African Publications Board. When I visited Namibia in 1987 and saw some of the many changes that had taken place during my absence, I thought it would be exciting to again do research in Namibia, but I had no idea how truly exciting it would be. I have had the opportunity to work on over twenty-five development-related projects, to do applied anthropology, to train Namibian students in social-science research, and to write the present book about Katutura. Without the encouragement and support of Debie LeBeau, I would have not been able to write it, and I would like to thank her for the considerable help she gave me. We often discussed the book during all the stages of preparation; she offered many suggestions and read the manuscript several times. I must also thank her for doing some of my work to enable me to work on the book and for being an understanding companion while I was writing it.

I want to thank Legio Skrywer and Jonas Katjarungu, who were my research assistants for the original fieldwork between 1967 and 1970. I did not want to name them in the previous book; now I feel there is no longer a need to keep their identity a secret. They took a certain risk by associating with me in those days; thanks for helping me. I would like to thank Chris Tapscott for inviting Debie and myself to work with the Namibian Institute of Social and Economic Research (now the Social Science Division of the University of

Namibia's Multi-Disciplinary Research Centre). The two years at the institute (1991–93) were exciting and challenging. Other institutional affiliations that I would like to acknowledge are my long-standing association with the University Centre for Studies in Namibia (TUCSIN); TUCSIN has assisted me in many ways over the years and I would like to express my appreciation for their support. BRICKS assisted me with the 1988 project, which was instrumental in renewing my contact with Namibia; my thanks to them for their assistance. I would like to thank other people who in different ways encouraged or supported my visits and research and shared their friendship with me: Jurgens Brand, Lourens Erasmus, Bruce and Allison Frayne, Peter Katjavivi, Johann and Gertrud Kenneweg, Carol and Dirk Kotzé, Rodian and Liz Kraus, Jan Limneos, Annelie Odendaal, Wolfgang Pandikow, Beatrice Sandelowsky, Christa and Manfred Schier, Martin and Val West, and Karl-Heinz and Maria Witt. To the other Namibians that I have known over the years I also want to say thanks for your interest, help, and support. Friendships in Namibia are special and people you meet are not easily forgotten. I hope to have the opportunity to do research, teach, and live in Namibia again in the near future.

During our research projects in Katutura and elsewhere, I had the pleasure of working directly with more than fifty Namibians, as enumerators, researchers, data-entry clerks, clients, and in other capacities. A special thanks to George Eiseb, Gotlieb Gowaseb, Felix Muyoba, Monica Ngajone, and Akiser Pomuti. You often explained and collected data for me; thanks for your help. If I still do not have the information correct, it is not your fault. You and others did your best to explain and describe events and concepts to me.

My thanks to the following people who read the manuscript, offered many valuable suggestions and suggested additional material for the book: Carol Kotzé, Phyllis Whitney, Chris Tapscott, Beatrice Sandelowsky, Annelie Odendaal, and Ben Fuller. The correct translation and orthography of African words were checked by Wilfrid Haacke, Joe Auala, Jekura Kavari, and P. Mbenzi. Peter Reiner made many editorial suggestions for the book; my sincere thanks to him for his careful and painstaking attention to detail. Ingrid van Graan at Gamsberg Macmillan also made many valuable suggestions and saw the book through the publication process. I would like to thank

Doreen Olivier and Margaret Paisley for word-processing part of the manuscript. Thanks to Eberhard Lisse for sending several drafts of the manuscript via electronic mail from Windhoek to San Diego; sending the files via EMAIL proved more difficult than expected, but in the end it did save considerable time and expense. Finally, I would like to acknowledge the leaves of absence I was granted by the San Diego State University.

Foreword

I have the pleasure to welcome the publication of Professor Wade Pendleton's book *Katutura: A Place Where We Stay*. Professor Pendleton deserves our congratulations for the manner in which he has dealt with the subject matter. He has not only provided us with an up-to-date depiction of socioeconomic conditions in Katutura, but has also managed to capture pivotal developments since independence.

Through this account we are reminded of the history of the Old Location, the tragic events which led to the December 1959 shooting and the circumstances under which Katutura was born. The crafting of Professor Pendleton's narrative has been done through careful research and is conveyed in a concise style that is sure to captivate its readers.

This is not just a balanced perspective of the history of Katutura based on historical accuracy, but also one that reflects a passion for the lives of the people who make up that history.

As we all know, Katutura was a home created for the people of the Old Location, to which they were forced to move. They in turn baptized this place Katutura, which means "we have no permanent dwelling-place." Since then, the people of Katutura have moved on through various stages of the liberation struggle. What they fought for and worked for over those years has been achieved.

Today, as Professor Pendleton testifies, Katutura is recognized as a significant suburb of the City of Windhoek. In a sense, Katutura has become unbound and transformed into what we might call "Matutura," meaning "a place where we stay."

DR. PETER H. KATJAVIVI

University of Namibia

Let Me Tell You This Story

There is a place called Katutura
in a Land of the Namibian
People called Nama, Damara
lived there and people
called Wambo, and Herero
came to stay with them
this was long before
this place called
Katutura existed

This was in a place called
the Old Location
Now the man called a boer
was putting himself on the throne
and when the people did rebel
his awful hand did slay many
in his brutal manner
and forced them to this awful
place

Divided they lived in this place
and worked themselves to poverty
Years came and went by
and the war of this humble
people was fought and won

People felt the peace
and their victor was
given the throne
poor as they are still
their hearts are warm
and will live with them
in this place called
Katutura

And this my friend
is the story of this
place called Katutura

Robert Harrison Isaacks
Windhoek, Namibia

1

Introduction

WINDHOEK IS the capital and major urban center of Namibia. Its history and development have much in common with other African towns and cities that came into being during the period of European colonialism in Africa. The German colonial administration and later the South African administration of the country was centered in Windhoek. My 1974 book, *Katutura: A Place Where We Do Not Stay,* was primarily about people who lived in Katutura, Windhoek's township for the indigenous African people. At the time of the study (1968–70), Namibia was called South West Africa by the government of the Republic of South Africa, which essentially administered the country as a fifth province of South Africa.[1] A major theme of the book was the extent to which the apartheid policies implemented in Windhoek and Katutura influenced the lives of the people who lived there. Beginning in 1979, and throughout the 1980s, most of the apartheid policies were abolished, and South West Africa eventually became an independent and sovereign country, Namibia, in March 1990. The present book is a comparative study of life in the Katutura township *before*, during the peak of the apartheid years (1968–70), and *now*, including the postindependence period (1988–93). Information for both periods comes from my fieldwork in Katutura, my participation in many research projects in Katutura and elsewhere in Namibia, and my long-standing interest in Katutura and Namibia.[2]

Three themes will be found in this book. The first is how postapartheid life in Katutura differs from life under apartheid. Freedom and independence from South Africa were welcomed by the people of Katutura, but not all the changes that have taken place have made life easier or better for them. A question related to the first theme is whether Katutura is a township that is being transformed into a suburb. I attempt to answer this question in the last chapter of the book. A second theme is the rapid urbanization that has taken place in Katutura over the last seven years. Katutura has experienced unprecedented growth in recent years, and characteristics associated with the urbanization/growth will be discussed. The third theme is stratification. The people and their households now exhibit much more socioeconomic diversity than they did previously. Many people are still very poor, others have become affluent, and there are those who are somewhere in between.

The book commences with a discussion of concepts and methodology. In chapter 2, the use of quantitative and qualitative data is reviewed. This book reports findings from many different research methods, and it is hoped that the pictures that emerge will help the reader understand life in Katutura. This is followed by a background chapter tracing the history of life in Windhoek's locations up to the move to Katutura. It is a story of indigenous African life in town, traced from the German colonial period up to the present. Katutura households and people are the subjects of the next two chapters, in which major research findings are reported. They are followed by chapters on urbanization and stratification that will discuss the findings in the context of these two themes. In the final chapter, life during and after apartheid is summarized and compared with the situation in South Africa and elsewhere. In most chapters, the reader will find individual case studies, usually in the respondent's own words, that report personal experiences pertaining to the topic under discussion.

In this study, "black people" refers to members of the indigenous "African" population, "coloured people" is the reference group term for people whose ancestry is both black and white, and "white people" are those of European ancestry. I have used both "black people" and "indigenous African people" interchangeably in the text. Where possible I have tried not to use racial terms from the apartheid era. All the terms are problematic at best. Many "black" people, such as the Nama, are in fact not at all black in skin color. Many "whites" are Africans, having been born in Africa, and in general people are increasingly sensitive about the inequality that these terms convey due to the apartheid era. When such racial terms are used, they are in lowercase to help minimize their importance; ethnic group terms such as "Herero" are in uppercase. Terms such as "non-white" or "non-black" are also only used when necessary. Ethnic and racial terminology has been used long enough to classify and reclassify people in order to exploit their labor and their lives. I am in full agreement with the position taken in *South African Keywords* (Boonzaier and Sharp *et al.* 1988), in which the editors and others comment on the objectionable nature of this terminology. At the same time, ethnic identities such as "Herero" or "Afrikaner" convey cultural and social information about the lifestyles of people who identify themselves by these names. Ethnic identity, like gender and age identities, are part of social identity, and attempts to suppress them are universally unsuccessful. Ethnic identity should be a source of pride for people and their children, not a category for discrimination or nationalism. The use or misuse of ethnicity in independent Namibia will only become apparent in the future.[3]

The title of the previous study, *Katutura: A Place Where We Do Not Stay*, reflected the opposition of many people to the forced move from the "old location" to Katutura.[4] Katutura was, indeed, a place where people did not *want* to stay, but where they were forced to stay following the enforcement of apartheid policies. Katutura was also a place where most people felt little permanent security about future residence; police or other authorities could force people to leave Katutura at any time. Today, people are staying in Katutura under different circumstances. Katutura today is a place where people can stay with more security and freedom than they could in the past. I considered calling this book "*Matutura: A Place Where We Can Stay*," but decided against it, even though the Herero word *matutura* means "a place where we can stay permanently," and I thought it would be a good title for the book. The people who live in Katutura never said they wanted their township to be called Katutura; the name was adopted by authorities who did not know what the name meant. If Katutura is to have a new name, the people who live there should decide what the new name is to be.[5]

Notes

1. When the period of South African or German control is under discussion, I refer to the country as South West Africa. In 1919, the League of Nations awarded South West Africa to South Africa to administer as a Class C Mandate. After the United Nations was formed in 1945, South Africa tried to annex the country and the United Nations resisted these attempts. The International Court of Justice at the Hague heard many cases relating to the South West Africa issue and eventually ruled that the United Nations General Assembly had the authority to revoke the mandate which it did (see Grotpeter 1994: 533–540). The international status of South West Africa was not really resolved until independence in 1990.

2. Where appropriate, I have taken material directly from my 1974 book, *Katutura: A Place Where We Do Not Stay.* Some material from my book and the research from that period has been rewritten, errors have been corrected, and in some cases the data was reanalyzed. When no reference for material is given in the text, it has been obtained from the 1974 book. In all other cases, the source is referenced.

3. Fosse (1992:3–4) makes a similar observation. He also comments that "the obvious South African abuse of the concepts or social phenomena of tribalism or ethnicity for the purpose of securing continued white domination . . . cannot justify the treating of ethnic factors as *merely* another neocolonial technique of domination, a view evident in much research on Namibia of the political economy school (for example, Melber 1985, Kandetu 1987, Lau 1988, Kaakunga 1990)." He continues to comment that there is a need for studies that do not simply fuel the unproductive debate as to whether ethnicity exists or not. He also comments that the problem is compounded because the people themselves continue to refer to themselves as "tribes" or "ethnic groups" despite the efforts of some social scientists and politicians to negate their social identities.

4. For more information on the name Katutura, see case study 3.

5. I would like to thank Joe Auala for making me aware of the implications of calling the book "Matutura."

2

The Social Science Perspective

Urban Anthropology and African Anthropology

How DOES THIS STUDY fit within modern urban anthropology? A collection of papers from a 1991 symposium devoted to the topic, "W(h)ither Urban Anthropology" sponsored by the Society for Urban Anthropology, provides some insight to answer the question. Breitborde (1994:3–9) identifies six themes that define modern urban anthropology: (1) there is no longer any debate about whether anthropology in the city is "anthropology"; (2) qualitative or quantitative research methods are equally appropriate; (3) nearly all urban anthropology studies take into account the wider cultural and social world to which the city belongs; (4) the most popular topics that urban anthropologists teach in their courses (and by inference want their students to read and learn about) include such long-standing interests of urban anthropologists as migration, social stratification, poverty, ethnicity, social organization, and applied topics; (5) the uniqueness of urban anthropology may be diminishing as anthropology becomes more generally urban and as such no longer needs the label urban; (6) the work of urban anthropologists has often influenced people in other disciplines but urban anthropology does not often get the credit. As is evident in other papers presented at the above-mentioned symposium, there is still considerable disagreement about how to define urban anthropology. However, the contribution and the activity of urban anthropology continues: "As anthropologists we continue to explore how people comprehend the places where they live; the conditions of their lives; how they may acquiesce to larger systemic factors, even while actively shaping meaning and order in their individual and community lives" (Breitborde 1994:8–9).

Katutura: A Place Where We Stay meets many of the parameters described above.[1] The quantitative and qualitative research methods used in the study are appropriate and more discussion on this topic is presented in the next section of this chapter. Some may say I have focused too narrowly on Katutura and not discussed more fully the wider Windhoek, Namibian, and regional social/cultural system. Perhaps it is a question of emphasis. A major theme of the study is how life for people in Katutura has changed since the days of formal apartheid. The change came from both outside and within. It was political, economic, and social, it was implemented at the international, national, and local level, and it had far-reaching effects on Katutura's people. The people of Katutura also protested and worked from within to do their part in making the changes happen. As I discuss in this book, Katutura in many ways is no longer a rigidly bounded social system as it was in the past. People today have the opportunity to enter or leave as their personal circumstances dictate. Just as life in the past was so heavily influenced by apartheid policies, life in Katutura today is influenced by government and municipal policies. Housing, employment, health, immigration policies, the changing political/economic situation in the new South Africa as well as a myriad of other factors, some more remote and others close at hand, influence life in Katutura today. Many of the most popular topics of urban anthropology are discussed in the book such as urbanization, poverty, stratification, ethnicity, social structure, and social history. I have tried to present both the diversity and similarity of the peoples of Katutura, to discuss the conditions of their lives, and to place that discussion within a sociocultural context. I view my study as part of urban anthropology, social anthropology, African studies, and more generally social science.

In a review of African anthropology, Moore (1994:122–32) has identified three themes that characterize modern African anthropology: ethnicity, social field, and identity. The theme of ethnic identity is well represented in the study in various ways: ethnic stereotyping, ethnic identity, characteristics of ethnic boundaries and how the boundaries have changed in recent years; social field is reflected in the various descriptions of the social/cultural context within which Katutura's people live and the various social settings described in the book; identity is discussed in the many ways in which Katutura people identify themselves, such as "city people," migrants, and the more affluent. My present study seems to touch all three themes albeit in a macro rather than a micro manner. I hope there is enough ethnographic content to satisfy the social anthropologists, enough urban issues for the urban anthropologists, and enough African context for the Africanists.

Gordon and Spiegel (1993:83–105) have recently reviewed the situation of anthropology in southern Africa. They comment, "little urban anthropology has been done" (Gordon and Spiegel 1993:94). Examples of urban research in South Africa include studies of kinship (Manona 1991), domestic gender relationships (van der Vliet 1991), children (Jones 1992 and Reynolds 1989), religion as a mechanism of social adjustment (Kiernan 1990), and the use of narratives in urban migration studies in Zambia (Ferguson 1990 and 1992). However, "there have been no anthropological studies of the role of cities in society" (Gordon and Spiegel 1993:95). Indeed, if research on high density rural settlements is excluded from their review of the literarure, only eleven references (8 percent of the total) to urban research are cited out of 137 references to anthropological research in recent years (Gordon and Spiegel 1993:95). Hopefully, *Katutura: A Place Where We Stay* will make a small contribution to fill a major gap in the southern Africa anthropological literature.

This book is based on data collected by means of various research methods, as well as my long period of association with Namibia and Katutura. I am of the opinion that qualitative methods (such as participant observation and ethnography) and quantitative methods (such as survey research) should complement each other. My view of social science is that *both* quantitative and qualitative approaches should be used in research and writing. The qualitative understanding of the social/cultural context provides the perspective that facilitates the interpretation of empirical findings from quantitative methods. Both methods are important and complement each other. But as Scrimshaw (1993:138)[2] recently wrote, "the debate over the relative merits of qualitative and quantitative methods rages on." I can report from my own experience that the debate for many is a *jihad*, and the intensity of some scholars' religious devotion to their preferred research method takes on the appearance of a crusade. The less one knows about the others' methods seems to be highly positively correlated with intolerance for those methods. I also refer the reader to a recent critique of the ethnographic (qualitative) method, *What's Wrong With Ethnography?* (Hammersley 1992:6), where the author comments that "I suggest that there is no general reason to believe that the findings of ethnography are any more valid than those of quantitative research."

The quantitative method, which makes use of survey research, is strongly represented in this book; this is not surprising, since I have been presenting workshops and conducting extensive survey research for over a decade. I have attempted to make use of the survey data with an understanding of its strengths and weaknesses. These strengths include the ability to select a representative sample population from which data may be generalized for the larger population: an important strength for urban research on a large, stratified population. The data collection may be fairly rapid, and it is replicable. For ease of data collection, coding, data entry, and analysis, most questions are closed, with preselected categories. Three crucial points need to be borne in mind as regards closed questions:

1. Questions and possible answers must be culturally and socially appropriate for those being interviewed.
2. Enumerators must be carefully trained in how to ask the questions.
3. Data-entry personnel must be trained to enter the data correctly.

Experience and skill significantly facilitate the analysis of the data. The rapid development of computers and software has made survey-data analysis a considerably easier task for those who are interested.

Not all the questions in a survey need to be closed with predetermined categories. I often include open questions in a specific format, the answers being listed by separate attributes or separate qualities. The coding of open-ended lists is time-consuming, but it is possible and often rewarding; however, there should be good reasons for leaving a question open. Pilot testing of surveys is essential. The better informed the researcher is about the population to be surveyed and the topics to be investigated, the more successful the survey will be. It has been a challenge to consult with experts who want to conduct a survey, know virtually nothing about survey research, and then proceed to tell the research consultant how to do the work. Surveys are excellent for revealing characteristics of a population, testing hypotheses, and sometimes making an unanticipated discovery.

What questions ought to be asked, what hypotheses are to be tested, what key questions require answers, and how does one gain the insight to ask these questions? Perhaps the greatest contribution social/cultural anthropology has made to the social sciences is to make people sensitive to the importance of context. An understanding of the social/cultural context is simply essential for good social-science research. During a recent Namibian nationwide survey, respondents were asked how many people eat the evening meal; unfortunately, one ethnic group does not have the concept of "meals" in its culture, and the question in that format was meaningless to them. Understanding context comes from experience, interest, knowledge, and an understanding of society. Anthropologists like to think that only they have the ability to understand context, and they often think it is gained only by years in the field. Sometimes it does take years, and sometimes it does not. The qualitative heavy ethnographic method has its strengths. Real versus ideal or normative behavior may be observed and recorded, delicate topics can be discussed, interrelationships may become apparent due to intense familiarity with the people and their views of the world, and perhaps the researcher is in a better position to evaluate and compare answers from informants. Intuition, hunches, insight, and ideas are often the result of the knowledge and understanding of the context within which people are living out the drama of their lives. But people also lie, hunches can be wrong, and ethnographers are well-known for the bias they have for their own people's point of view. Combining both qualitative and quantitative methods affords social scientists the best opportunity of investigating the difficult human problems we are so fond of studying.

Data Used in This Book

Details of surveys referred to in the text are listed in appendixes 1 and 2. The primary dataset for Katutura now is the 1991 Katutura Survey (KAT1991); other datasets are the Household Health and Nutrition Survey (HHNS), the Health and Daily Living Survey (HDL), the NBC Radio Listeners Survey (RADIO), the War-Affected People Survey (WAP), and the Energy Usage Survey (ENERGY). The various datasets are referred to in the text by these abbreviations. KAT1991 provides information on households and people. Details about qualitative data for Katutura before are discussed in appendix 1, under the informant sample information. For Katutura now, a number of case studies were collected from informants representative of old and new Katutura, migrants, types of households, and other topics. The households were chosen from the KAT1991 to be representative of their category or type. The household was located from the KAT1991 survey map, and the household head was contacted. One of my research assistants or I returned to the selected households and asked if we could collect additional information. Some of these people were interviewed a number of times over the period between 1991 and 1993. The additional in depth data was collected from people in households that were selected to be representative of both Katutura and of the type of household or personal category (for example, migrant or female-centered household head). The selection of households and informants in this manner is possibly an innovative method. My long-term familiarity with Katutura and the people who live there provides my personal perspective for the interpretation and analysis of the information presented.

Twelve case studies or vignettes are presented in this book. These short case studies are not typical anthropological case studies; they are short personal descriptions of circumstances or experiences in the old Main Location, or Katutura. Some are based on interviews with people who are representative of household types or categories of people as described above, while others are taken from published material describing significant events or circumstances. When selecting material for these case studies, I attempted to afford the reader the opportunity to understand what the people themselves say about events and circumstances that influence their lives. As Melber (1988:16) comments in the introduction to *Katutura—Alltag im Ghetto*, it is also necessary for the people themselves to say in their own words how they perceive their situation.

In case study 1 for instance, I discuss the problems of data collection in Katutura before and now.

CASE STUDY 1: Fieldwork in Katutura Before and Now[3]

Doing fieldwork in Katutura in the 1960s was difficult. Many of the difficulties experienced in conducting fieldwork in South Africa were also present in Namibia, but there were additional problems. The international status of Namibia was under review by the United Nations and the World Court at The Hague. Whites were generally suspicious of foreigners, and I was suspected by some of spying for the United Nations. At the same time, some suspected I had connections with the South African government. Both extremes of suspicion reflected the prevailing political climate. Among the African population, there was considerable resentment of the South African government and municipal authorities who enforced apartheid policies. In the late 1960s, the recommendations of the Odendaal Commission to formalize apartheid in Namibia were rigorously implemented, and the country was administered like a fifth province of South Africa.

At the beginning of my 1960s research, people declined to be interviewed, and some were even openly hostile. Several times, the security police contacted people whom I had interviewed, and people were hesitant to be interviewed while such interference continued. In the Old Windhoek Main Location, I had difficulty talking to Herero people until I explained my research to Clemens Kapuuo and he granted me permission to talk to the people. Over time, as people became more used to my presence, interaction and interviews became somewhat easier. There were other difficulties, however. The Windhoek main "location," located to the west of the central business district, was finally closed by the municipal authorities in 1968, and the people were forced to move to Katutura under protest. People were experiencing much hardship, and an inquiring anthropologist was not always welcome.

I remember how the Old Location impressed me. Most houses were built with metal sheeting (called sinks[4]) and one had the impression of a shanty town. There were hills and many trees. Houses looked shabby and not very substantial at first glance. But first impressions can be deceptive. Inside, many had finished walls that were sometimes covered with burlap, nice furniture, and a comfortable homey feeling. Because people built their own houses, they could be enlarged as necessary to accommodate new family members. Rooms could be constructed and rented out. Houses could also be inherited. I remember people sitting on their porch in the evening entertaining visitors, Herero women sitting on the ground in front of their homes sewing dresses with old hand-cranked sewing machines, and night school for adults who wanted to learn English after working all day.

Several different types of data were collected during the 1960s research. One database was an opportunity sample of 100 informants interviewed by me and my two research assistants. It was not possible to survey the township in any systematic or random manner owing to the suspicion and even hostility with which interviews with strangers were met. Advance scheduling of interviews was necessary, and usually a friend or relative of the subject sponsored me. I did have opportunities to meet informally with key informants and attend social activities in Katutura. An offer to take free wedding photographs brought many wedding invitations. But it was never easy to move about in Katutura and be inconspicuous. I relied heavily on my two research assistants, for the research would not have been successful without their help and goodwill. They made introductions, explained people's behavior, arranged interviews and invitations to parties, and explained my presence.

In the 1960s, the presence of an anthropologist asking questions and seeking interviews with people was a strange and unusual phenomenon. Perhaps due to the difficulties I experienced in interviewing people, I made extensive use of public records. Surveys were conducted of employment contracts, Katutura housing records and visitors' permits, travel pass records, magistrate and church records, and municipal reports. It appears obvious now, but it was not so clear then, that the extensive use of these records was a result of the difficulty of interacting with people. Katutura and Windhoek were part of a rigidly stratified society where apartheid was enforced with even greater effectiveness than in South Africa.

My current fieldwork in Katutura commenced in 1988 with the HDL Project (Pendleton 1990b). Since then, I have worked on about twenty-five applied development projects in Namibia, many of which included Katutura for data collection. The ability to conduct many data collection projects in Katutura, both quantitative and qualitative, reflects the changes in the social and political climate there. It is much easier to conduct interviews and visit people now than it was in the past, and many students and members of the public are eager to work on social science projects. With my colleague Debie LeBeau, I have trained more than fifty Namibians in data collection, data entry, data clean-up, and data analysis. The atmosphere of suspicion and mistrust so prevalent in Katutura in the past has been replaced by cooperation, assistance, and interest. The same cannot be said for the rest of Windhoek and Namibia. Windhoek whites were difficult to survey in 1988 (on the HDL) and they were difficult in 1992 (on the NBC); many were suspicious, uncooperative, and sometimes even hostile. As one Caprivian said after quitting the project: "I can be abused by my own people, I don't need to be abused by those whites too." Another fieldworker said: "Big dogs and high fences make it impossible to say, 'Hello, my name is . . . .'" People in communal areas are nearly always cooperative, but they increasingly demand to see some results from "all the surveys."

Comparisons

The reader will find several types of comparisons in this book. A major comparative theme is Katutura before (1968–70) and Katutura now (1991–93). When referring to Katutura before, I have tried to be consistent and use the past tense; when reference is made to Katutura now, the present tense is used. Other comparisons are made between old and new Katutura, household types, and households above and below the median household income level.

Old and New Katutura

Comparisons are made between old Katutura and new Katutura. Old Katutura was developed during the apartheid era (between 1950 and 1979), while new Katutura was developed from 1980 onwards. Although independence from South Africa did not occur until 1990, much of the apartheid legislation was abolished in the 1980s. The old and new Katutura comparison reflects different degrees of apartheid influence that can still be seen today, such as the greater ethnic homogeneity in the former "ethnic sections" of old Katutura. Other differences exist in socioeconomic characteristics of old and new Katutura.

Household Types

Information on households headed by males and females is given. Households headed by males include those conjugal households formed around a nuclear or extended family as well as households without the 'conjugal' relationship. Female-headed households, also not based on a conjugal relationship, are also discussed. Comparisons between households based on conjugal and non-conjugal unions are provided.

Above and Below the Household Median Income

Comparisons are made between households that are above and below the median monthly household income. The median divides the population at the fiftieth percentile; that is, it separates those above and below the midpoint in the distribution. The median household income is very close to the Household Subsistence Level (HSL) for the period under discussion (see Potgieter for a detailed discussion of the interpretation of the HSL), and, in a *relative* sense, separates households that are *below* a minimum subsistence level from those that are *above* this level. It is important to note that the HSL is not the same as the Household Effective Level (HEL), which is 150 percent of the HSL figure. The HSL researchers have found after numerous studies that although the HSL reflects "the cost of a *theoretical budget* of necessities, it does not suggest an adequate *income* because in practice, out of a total income equivalent to that budget, one third will be diverted away from the specified items to other immediate essentials" (Potgieter n.d.:7). Therefore, the HEL is in reality the figure that should be used for a minimum household budget or poverty datum line.

The HSL, like various other measures of relative subsistence or poverty, has both its strengths and its weaknesses. Wilson and Ramphele (1989:16) comment that, "as Beckerman has cryptically observed, it does not really make sense to define poverty at some minimum level when people continue to survive below it." They also comment on the danger of misuse of such statistics to prove or disprove some hypothesis. However, I want to make use of the HSL to evaluate some relative differences in Katutura households.

HSL surveys have been conducted by the Institute for Planning Research at the University of Port Elizabeth, South Africa, since 1973. Major urban centers in South Africa and Namibia are surveyed every six months. The HSL is calculated on the basis of the current local cost of food, clothing, fuel, lighting, cleansing materials, rent, and transport for a household of six people consisting of two adults, two teenage children and two preteenage children (Potgieter n.d.:16–25). I have used the published HSL data for September 1991 for Windhoek blacks.

Notes

1. In my previous book I devoted many pages to the discussion of 'theoretical issues' such as what is urban anthropology, Mitchell's situational analysis, Barth's formulation of ethnicity, and an extensive discussion of class and caste concepts. There is no discussion of "what is urban anthropology" or situational analysis in the present book, and the discussion of caste is minimal and is used primarily when reference is made to Katutura before. West (1987:x) also comments in his revised study of Port Nolloth that he decided not to include a theoretical discussion of caste and class.

2. The article by Scrimshaw reflects my own approach to both anthropological and social-science research. I have made use of her formulation of the qualitative/quantitative debate.

3. I published a similar paper under the title "Fieldwork in Katutura,

Namibia: Two Different Research Experiences" (Pendleton 1990a). When I wrote that article, the 1988 fieldwork in Katutura had been completed, and I was pleased that it had gone so well. The following year, we were unable to complete the fieldwork among whites in Windhoek owing to their uncooperative attitude. The dataset had to be weighted to take into account the approximately 50 percent of Windhoek interviews that had to be canceled.

4. Probably a corrupt form of the Afrikaans *sinkplaat* (sheet of corrugated iron).

3

Background

Namibia: Regions and People

NAMIBIA, WITH A 1991 population of about 1.5 million people, is one of Africa's most sparsely populated countries, and about half of this population live in the northern one-fifth of the country. The small population size does not mean that the country is homogeneous and easy to understand. On the contrary, diversity and complexity characterize the Namibian population. Windhoek, as the capital and largest urban center, has attracted people from all over the country, and Windhoek's African township, Katutura, has experienced significant urban migration in recent years. The people come from a diversity of backgrounds and they have been influenced by a variety of forces of change. Briefly described below are profiles of the various regions of the country and characteristics of the people found in these regions (refer to Map A for the location of the regions).

Rural Communal Area Dwellers

Rural communal areas in the country are home to about 70 percent of the population, but they only occupy about 40 percent of the land (Vaughn 1993:64).[1] These areas are characterized by the lack of individual land ownership. Permission to occupy land must usually be obtained from a chief, headman, or other local authority. People living in these areas share a high degree of cultural similarity and linguistic homogeneity. They have the security and solidarity of living in communities of people who are often closely related, will assist in time of need, share the successes and failures of everyday life, and provide social support on an almost daily basis. The social structure within the communal areas is characterized by households made up of couples with children and other relatives. Within all of these areas non-couple based households consisting of a woman, her children, and relatives are also common, making up as much as 30 percent of all households in some Regions such as Kavango (Yaron et al. 1992:15), Onaanda in central Owambo (Botelle 1992:37), and the Eastern Communal Areas (Iken et al. 1994:32). On the other hand, people in these communal rural areas have fewer jobs in both the formal and informal sectors of the economy, fewer opportunities for formal education and vocational training, and they have less access to modern media. When rural communal dwellers migrate to Katutura looking for jobs they usually approach the job market with a serious handicap.

Very little development took place in these rural communal areas during the period of German colonialism (1890–1915) and South African occupation (1915–89), and access to and from these areas was tightly controlled. Africans wanting to travel to other areas of Namibia usually had to have travel passes and/or employment contracts. Especially in the northern regions of the country bordering Angola, the effects of the Namibian War for Independence (approximately 1968–89) had considerable impact on people's lives. About 40,000 Namibians went into exile, many of whom became combatants and fought for Namibia's independence primarily along the Namibia/Angola border. There were frequent military patrols by the South African Defense Force and the South West African Territorial Force, which often harassed the local population; there was a curfew on nighttime travel, and many people were relocated within the northern regions. After independence and the return to Namibia of those who had lived in exile, many people were found to have stress and work-related problems because of the war (Preston et al 1993). The ability to relocate to Windhoek was highly controlled. However, beginning in the 1980s and especially after independence in 1990, people were free to travel and migrate to new places and many people took advantage of that opportunity to move to Katutura.

Each rural communal area has one or more peri-urban or urban areas with some infrastructure such as schools, post office, shops, radio station, police station, piped water system, and electricity. They are referred to as peri-urban because most lack the formal structure of a municipality; some of these areas have been incorporated as municipalities. People who want to live a more modern lifestyle and/or want to leave the more remote rural communal way of life, move to these peri-urban areas. They still live in communities of people who are culturally and linguistically similar to themselves, but they have opportunities for alternative lifestyles. Others live in these areas for a while and then move to other parts of Namibia including Katutura.

Described below are some basic features of the major communal areas in the country. The largest rural population is the Oshiwambo-speaking people who make up about 45 percent of the Namibian population. They live in north-central Namibia primarily in the four regions of Omusati, Ohangwena, Oshana, and Oshikoto. They live in dispersed homesteads of extended families (not in villages) cultivating millet, corn, and keeping cattle. From the air, the country of the Owambo is easily recognized by its flat terrain and the enclosed palisade homesteads made up of many separate huts and houses for specialized activities. The two largest urban settlements in Owambo are Oshakati and Ondangwa where about 6 percent of the area's people live more modern lifestyles in modern houses or shanty settlements, own televisions, and pursue informal sector entrepreneurial activities as well as formal employment in the government and private sector (Pendleton et al. 1992).

To the east of Owambo in the Okavango Region reside five closely related Kavango ethnic groups who are also matrilineal in social structure and speak a Bantu language (Kangwali). The people of the Kavango region make up about 10 percent of the nation's population. These people typically live in villages situated along the south bank of the Okavango River, which forms the boundary between Angola and Namibia. They are settled horticulturalists and fishermen and they also keep livestock. Rundu is the largest urban settlement in the area where about 15 percent of the region's population live. A recent study identified a number of major problems affecting the population, including the need for an improved water supply, improved health care and education facilities, reduction in poverty, better household food security, and improved transport services (Yaron et al. 1992:212). Such problems are typical of the rural communal areas of Namibia and many people leave the rural areas and migrate to the towns because of these problems.

In the eastern Caprivi live the Mafwe and Masubiya, who speak Silozi (a Bantu language), and live in villages. They cultivate millet and corn, fish, but keep less livestock in part due to the presence of the tsetse fly. The Mafwe and Masubiya are culturally and linguistically closely related to other people found in the adjacent countries of Zambia, Zimbabwe, Angola, and Botswana. The Caprivi population make up about 5 percent of the Namibian population and the urban residents of Katima Mulilo (the Regional center) make up about 20 percent of the area's population.

In the north-eastern part of Otjozondupa Region is "Bushman-land" where some Bushmen live in the administrative center at Tsumkwe and others have relocated to cattle posts where they pursue new economic activities funded in part by foreign donor organizations, the most prominent of which is the Nyae Nyae Development Foundation of Namibia. Few if any Bushmen are able to pursue a hunting and gathering way of life today and modern social anthropological and historical research has suggested that some hunting and gathering groups in the past may also have kept livestock. Many of the myths and misconceptions surrounding the identity of Bushmen are discussed by Gordon (1992). A more general ethnographic account that also deals with change is Lee (1993). Bushmen are speakers of non-Bantu click languages (Khoisan languages), one of the most prominent being !Kung. The economic and political interests of some of these people are represented today by a Bushman Farmer's Union.

To the west of the Owambo, in the Kunene Region, are found the Himba, who are nomadic pastoralists, with their herds of cattle and goats. They live in villages and follow a rather conservative rural lifestyle strongly influenced by their traditions. The area where they live is remote and not easily accessible, and they have been influenced somewhat less by events of the twentieth century than other people in Namibia. The reader should not however think that the Himba remained untouched by the events of the last two decades in Namibia. Many of their villages were relocated because of the war. Military patrols also interfered with their way of life. The drought in 1992 reduced the size of many herds causing a loss of wealth. Some Himba have moved to the regional center at Opuwo where a more settled urban life is possible. The Bushmen and Himba people make up about 2 percent of the population of Namibia.

In the eastern and southern parts of Omaheke and central Otjozondupa regions are the Eastern Communal Areas populated by Otji-herero-speaking people making up about 3 percent of the Namibian population. Within these areas, people live in dispersed homesteads on farms or cattle posts and in urban settlements. The largest urban settlement is Okakarara with about 9 percent of the area's population. Cattle ranching is the primary economic activity of the Herero. Herero cultural traditions are respected by most of the rural people; however, as a group they are much less conservative than the Himba (who also speak Otjiherero, a Bantu language). Cattle are often sold at auction for cash to meet household expenses and many people purchase basic food stocks from rural shops. About a third of households in the area have access to trucks or motor cars which makes transport to and from the rural areas easier (Iken et al. 1994:43,48).

In addition to the Bushmen, two other Namibian ethnic groups who speak a non-Bantu language are the Damara and the Nama (both speak Nama). In the western Erongo and south-central areas of the Kunene regions are dispersed farm settlements of Damara people. They are primarily livestock ranchers many of whom live on farms purchased by the old South West African Administration and allocated to Damara people who wanted to live in the area. Small livestock, (especially goats), farming, and very limited crop cultivation are the primary economic activities. Many households are supported by pensions and remittances from family members living outside the area. The population of the area is about 3 percent of the country's population. The administrative center of this area is located at Xhorixas where about 40 percent of the area's population live.

The last communal areas to be mentioned are in the south of the country located in the central-southern Hardap and central Karas regions, inhabited primarily by Nama people. These areas are collectively referred to as the Southern Communal Areas and include Namaland, Bondelswarts, Neuhof, and Warmbad. They are sparsely populated, receive very little rain, are extremely dry, support no dry crop agriculture, and have frequent droughts. Settlements of one or more homesteads are concentrated at water points and some households relocate due to water availability. Households support themselves by keeping goats and sheep, by means of pensions, and remittances from those living elsewhere. About 1 percent of the Namibian population are found in the Southern Communal Areas with about 20 percent of the area's population in the administrative center at Gibeon.

The Commercial Farming Area

From the southern part of Oshikoto Region in the north, to Karas Region in the south, Omaheke Region in the east, and Erongo in the west is located the commercial farming area of Namibia. Within this area are over 3,000 farms owned primarily by Afrikaner and German Namibians that cover about 40 percent of the available land area of the country. The commercial farming area population is about 6 percent of the total Namibian population. Each farm has one or more farm worker families of black Namibians who live/work on the farm. Life on the farms in the commercial farming area is not easy for black Namibians employed there; they work long hours, have limited social interaction with people outside the farm, have limited opportunities for educating their children, and limited prospects of improving the quality of their lives. The ethnicity of many farm workers is Damara. The commercial farming sector has long received substantial technical and financial support from the previous government. Commercial cattle, sheep, and crop cultivation (in the Tsumeb-Grootfontein-Otavi farming area) are major economic activities of the area, and they make a significant contribution to the gross domestic product of the country.[2] South of Windhoek, within the commercial farming area, is the former Rehoboth District which had a special status in the pre-independence era. It was the only area where non-whites had the right to individual freehold land ownership. Most people in this area are Rehoboth "Basters," a coloured ethnic group whose ancestors moved into the area from South Africa in 1879 (Grotpeter 1994:430). Livestock products are marketed locally as well as exported to South Africa and Europe. The commercial farming area is another sector of the country from which people leave and migrate to the towns including Windhoek.

The Towns of Namibia

Within the same regions as the commercial farming area of the country are located the small towns of Namibia. There are sixteen small towns with populations of 5,000 or more people inhabited by about 13 percent of the Namibian population. Windhoek with a population of about 150,000 has almost as many people as all the other towns combined. Rehoboth, Swakopmund, Grootfontein, and Keetmanshoop with populations of around 20,000 each are the largest towns after Windhoek. They all have a similar postapartheid urban geographical structure. The German and Afrikaner households are located in housing areas near the central business district of the town, these households have modern houses with electricity, water, and most modern conveniences. Some black households with wage earners who have good government or private sector employment also live in these housing areas. However, most blacks live in the township in low-cost housing, and in some cases squatter communities. Blacks have migrated to these towns seeking work and/or alternative lifestyles just as many have migrated to Windhoek.

Windhoek, with its substantially larger economy and population, greater opportunities, and greater promise, has always been a magnet attracting people from all over the country. People have migrated to Windhoek from the rural communal areas, the commercial farming area, and other towns. In the next section of this chapter the settlement and development of Windhoek is described.

People Come to Town

Settlement and Development of Windhoek

The Herero call Windhoek *Otjomuise* (steaming place), and the Nama call it |Ae||gams (hot springs), after the hot springs which are found there. In 1842, about 2,000 people were living in the Windhoek area under the Oorlam[3] leader Jonker Afrikaner (Lau 1987:33). The name Windhoek, in a slightly altered form, is attributed to Jonker Afrikaner. Kotzé (1990:3) states that Jonker Afrikaner chose Windhoek for a settlement so that he could be near the large Herero cattle herds he regularly raided. Jonker Afrikaner left the Windhoek area in 1852, but the area remained occupied by Herero and Damara who planted maize and other crops near the hot springs. The mission station and school were reestablished by Rhenish missionaries in March 1871. In 1880, Windhoek was raided by Herero from Okahandja who found the area deserted, and they destroyed the mission station and other buildings. The area remained unoccupied until the arrival of the German *Schutztruppe* (occupation forces) (Kotzé 1990:2–7).

The modern beginnings of Windhoek date from October 1890 with the arrival of *Schutztruppe* under the command of Curt von François and the construction of a fort (Mossolow 1965:116–7). The German occupation of Windhoek led to a new type of settlement in the area. Blacks were employed by the *Schutztruppe* to help in the construction of the fort and other buildings, and as servants. In 1894, Windhoek had 85 white civilians (including five women), about 500 members of the *Schutztruppe*, and 300–400 blacks, who were mostly Damara (Mossolow 1965:139). The large number of Damara probably reflects the fact that some, having lived in subservience to and fear of the Herero and Nama, welcomed the opportunity to escape by coming to Windhoek. A new kind of warfare struck South West Africa between 1904 and 1906. Three wars were fought between the German *Schutztruppe* and the indigenous African peoples. These wars were disastrous for the Bondelswarts Nama, the Herero led by Samuel Maharero, and the Nama led by Hendrik Witbooi. The Germans won all three wars with the loss of only 1,626 men (Hintrager 1955:73). The losses by and consequences for the black people, on the other hand, were devastating. Bley (1971:150–51) estimates that about 50,000 or 75

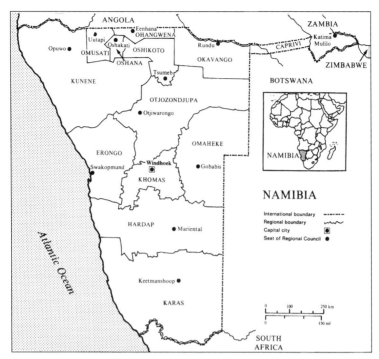

Map A: Namibia and Africa

percent–80 percent of the Herero population perished, while about 7,000 or 35 percent of the Nama population died. The Damara, who were often caught in the middle, may have lost as many as 17,000 people. The exact number of Herero and others who died during these wars has come under review in recent years. Pool (1991:278–80), writing about the Herero, states that it is impossible to determine the exact number who died because the number of Herero alive before the war is not known with certainty; he reports numbers that vary from 23,000 to 73,000. Although the exact number of people who died in thcse wars is in dispute, the magnitude of the impact on African life cannot be overemphasized.

The terrible defeat of the Herero can be ascribed largely to the ruthless strategies of the German Lieutenant-General Lothar von Trotha and the superior firepower of the German troops. Many Herero fled to Botswana, where they and their descendants still live in the Ngamiland region. Ngamiland Herero were allowed to resettle in Namibia only after Namibia's independence. Those who survived the conflicts and remained in South West Africa were deprived of their right to own property, including cattle, which was the central feature of the economy and culture for the Nama and especially the Herero. People had no alternative but to go to the towns and farms and work for the Germans. The black population of Windhoek doubled between 1903 and 1912, and the Herero population increased fivefold. Mossolow (1965:117) states that people who came to Windhoek to work for the Germans received food and clothing as wages and lived near building sites in separate ethnic communities, probably due to the history of frequent conflicts between the various groups. Wagner (1951:89) mentions that during this time blacks lived in huts that were scattered all over the town. According to a map of Windhoek in von François (1899:92), however, locations were beginning to develop as early as 1892.

Location Life Begins

Separate places called "locations," in which the indigenous African population lived apart from whites, have been part of the urban geography of Windhoek ever since the late nineteenth century. Some of the early Windhoek "locations" were occupational in character. The *Truppenwerft* and the *Polizeiwerft* were for those employed by the *Schutztruppe* and the police, respectively, while other people lived in huts throughout the town and in its vicinity (Wagner 1951:89). *Werft* is the locally-used German word for location, called *lokasie* in Afrikaans. The Nama word ǂNūkhoeǁgâub (black people's place) is especially descriptive. In 1912, the Windhoek Town Council established the Main Location west of town, and a location in Klein Windhoek, a suburb east of the center of town. In 1913, blacks living in various parts of the Windhoek area were moved to these new locations. The different black ethnic groups, apparently by choice, settled in different parts of these locations, and occupational locations ceased to exist.

Following the defeat of the German troops in South West Africa in 1915, the government of the Union of South Africa took over the administration of South West Africa and Windhoek. From that time on, black affairs were administered much as in South Africa, and the locations were placed under a municipal superintendent of locations. The South African government retained the locations as they were, since this paralleled their own policies. In 1932, the Main Location was reorganized, straight streets were laid out, and ethnic group sections formally established. The people in the locations apparently accepted the formal establishment of ethnic sections. The Damara, Nama, and Owambo referred to their sections by the municipal administrative designations such as Damara Two or Owambo One.[4] The Herero had already adopted the practice of dividing their section of the Main Location into smaller subdivisions of their own, naming them either after a place or an important person. One of these divisions was called *Otjikatjamuaha*, the place of Chief Tjamuaha's people, while another was called *Otjimaruru*, the place of the people from Omaruru. Herero people explained the development of these named divisions as follows: As the Herero came to Windhoek, they settled in groups that corresponded roughly to the various places from where they came or the particular chief whose authority they acknowledged. Over time, the various parts of the Herero section came to be known by these terms. By the 1960s, these designations were no longer of much significance, especially since most of the chiefs had been killed during the war against the Germans and many important Herero places had been taken over by whites. However, the designations had not been forgotten by the people. In 1968, I was able to walk around the Main Location with an assistant and trace the boundaries of the various Herero subdivisions on a map by asking people the name of the area in which they lived.[5]

When the Main Location was reorganized, each block was divided into residential plots rented from the municipality for about R0.10 per month.[6] At the time, all housing in the location was built by the people themselves. It generally comprised square and rectangular houses made of wooden frames and walls of flattened metal (corrugated iron) on the outside and sacking or clay on the inside. This was the most common type of housing in the location until the opening of Katutura in 1959. These houses were of great economic and personal importance to the people. They represented property, for many people their most valuable asset, which could be sold, rented, and inherited. Often, extra rooms were added and rented out to supplement the owner's monthly income.

Control of the locations was the responsibility of the municipality, but efforts were made to involve residents in the administration of the locations. An Advisory Board, consisting of twelve non-white members under the chairmanship of the white location superintendent, was established in the Main Location in 1927. There were representatives for the Damara, Herero, Owambo, and Coloured section of the Main Location. There was also a representative for the Union Section (a section for people from the "Union"), which was composed primarily of people from South Africa and elsewhere. Half the members of the Board were elected by the residents, while the remaining members were appointed by the location superintendent; elections were held when there were vacancies. Some groups did not succeed in electing a member of their ethnic section, either on account of their small numbers or because they voted for candidates of other ethnic groups. In such a case, the location superintendent would appoint the candidate from that section who had received the most votes to the board. The result was that each section was represented by one or more members from its own ethnic group, irrespective of whether the section's members had voted for candidates of other ethnic groups. The most frequently discussed topics at board meetings were health, sanitation, education, and the operation of the board (Wagner 1951:115). A subject that was periodically discussed was heavy drinking, illegal brewing, and illegal selling of alcoholic beverages. In what must have been a forerunner of the Advisory Board, the foremen had already complained in German times about the problems they were experiencing on account of heavy drinking.

In 1947, the municipality decided to increase the number of migrant Owambo contract workers (Owambo men on a work contract for a specified period of time) in Windhoek and built a compound for them. This location was called the *Pokkiesdraai* Contract Owambo Compound. By 1955, there were as many contract Owambo as resident town Owambo, who now numbered more than 1,700 people.[7] Although town Owambo had chosen to remain in Windhoek permanently and had in many cases renounced their claim to land rights in Owambo, they still recognized the elite status of Owambo chiefs. When these chiefs came to Windhoek and other towns in South West Africa, town Owambo would fall on their knees before them, give them presents and hold celebrations in their honor. These customs, however, were no longer followed in the 1960s. Possibly, they ceased because Owambo people in town had lived away from Owambo too long, and many of the 1960s' generation were born in town and had never been to Owambo. It could also be due to the fact that some chiefs were too closely associated with the apartheid administration of the South African government; some were appointed and others actively cooperated with the administration.

During the 1950s the Windhoek municipality, in consultation with the South West Africa Administration and the South African government, decided to build a new location northwest of Windhoek and move all location residents there. The subject had been under discussion ever since the 1920s, but construction only commenced during the mid-1950s. The relocation of people was considered necessary because the town had expanded westward to such an extent that it reached the edge of the Main Location, thus bringing whites and non-whites into closer proximity. The municipality wanted to move the non-white people farther out of town and use the land thus vacated for white residential *erven* (lots). They also considered the Main Location to be a shantytown and a breeding-place for disease where people were living in substandard housing without adequate sanitation facilities. The new location was supposed to provide better housing with sanitation facilities.

Most Main Location residents opposed the planned closure of the Main Location and refused to consider moving to Katutura, the proposed new location. Complaints centered around the increased cost of Katutura housing, the loss of houses that were their own property, and the greater distance between the location and town. Opposition to the move reached a climax in December 1959. A group of Herero women made a protest march to the administrator's residence on December 3. Five days later saw an effective boycott against municipally operated facilities such as buses, the beer hall, and the cinema. On the night of December 10, a protest meeting held in the Main Location developed into a confrontation with the police. The police shot and killed eleven people and some forty-four required medical attention[8] (Goldblatt 1971:262; Hall 1961:3). Immediately after the confrontation, between 3,000 and 4,000 people fled the location and refused to return because they were afraid of further trouble. Many "asked" (according to the Katutura location superintendent) to be allowed to move to Katutura, and the authorities agreed to this, despite the fact that Katutura had not yet been completed. About 3,000 people subsequently took up residence in Katutura, which undoubtedly pleased the authorities. It is clear, however, that most people moved out of fear of further shootings by the police and military.

The Old Location was officially closed on August 31, 1968. Many Herero and Damara, guided by their political leaders, remained behind in the Old Location until the very last week, saying that they would never move. Political opposition to the move represented a protest against the application of the South African government's apartheid policies to South West Africa and the Windhoek municipality's implementation of those policies. Eventually, however, all people in the Old Location, with the exception of about 300 people who decided to go to their reserves (communal areas), moved to Katutura without further incident. Previously, in 1961, the residents of the Klein Windhoek location had also been moved to Katutura, and in 1963 *Pokkiesdraai* was closed and the Owambo contract workers were moved to a new compound inside Katutura. The very name, Katutura, became a symbol for opposition to the forced move and more generally to the implementation of apartheid policies in South West Africa.

With the closure of the locations, especially the Main Location, and the move to Katutura, an era in township life came to an end. A number of activities had already ceased to exist even before the Main Location was closed, probably on account of the tension and suspicion surrounding the closure. Among the clubs and activities that came to an end before 1959 were the Bunga Private Club, which had been started in 1936 (a burial, mutual aid, and social club); the African Improvement Society, established for educational and social improvement purposes; the non-white Railway Staff Association, which might have been a forerunner of a railway workers trade union; the Hakahana Turf Club, which sponsored popular horse races; a Boy Scout troop; the "tribal court"; and the brass bands that each ethnic group section used to have (Wagner 1951:125–31, 273, 275). Advisory Board elections drew 38 percent of the population in 1948, and there was active campaigning using rubber-stamped and mimeographed handbills with candidates' names. On election day, a loudspeaker van advertised candidates' names and a truck took people to the polls (Wagner 1951:108); there were never any Advisory

Board elections in Katutura. In the 1992 regional and local elections in independent Namibia, 25,924 Katutura people voted, which is about 63 percent of the 1991 adult Katutura population. This is an obvious indication of the importance the Katutura population attaches to voting.

The confrontation over the move to Katutura corresponds to the beginning of political parties. The greater political awareness among people resulted in a diminishing interest in the Advisory Board. Several former members of the Advisory Board (for example, Clemens Kapuuo), became leaders of political parties that opposed the government. They refused to be identified with institutions such as Advisory Boards that implemented apartheid policies. When the Afrikaner-oriented National Party came to power in 1948 and implemented the segregationist policies even more rigorously under the apartheid system, this created an atmosphere in which people belonging to clubs and associations were suspected of antigovernment activities. Consequently, clubs and other activities that had been features of social life in the Old Location ceased to exist. After the shootings in the Main Location, Sam Nujoma left the country in 1960 to go into exile—to return only some three decades later to become the first president of an independent Namibia. Clemens Kapuuo was assassinated in 1978, but others who were politically active then and later (both "stayers" and "returnees"[9]) have now taken leading roles in SWAPO, the DTA, and other political parties.

In Case Study 2 below, John Ya-Otto describes life in the Old Location. This vivid account affords the reader a glance at the community and lifestyle that had evolved in the Old Location over the many decades of its existence.

CASE STUDY 2: Life in the Old Main Location[10]

It was easy to be mistaken about the Old Location. Vast, crowded, the shanty town wrapped itself around the scrubby hills of Windhoek's northern fringe, on the opposite side of the city from the white suburbs. The wiry shrubs gave way to houses made of cardboard, cloth, scraps of plywood, flattened oil drums and other makeshift building materials, thrown together in no apparent order. Only when you got near could you distinguish the shacks, set so close together that some families could easily touch their neighbours' walls from their own windows. Family quarrels behind the thin, gaping walls soon became neighbourhood gossip. Everyone knew one another and strangers did not remain so for long. You knew the streets, unmarked and unnamed, only after you had lived in the Old Location for a long time. Around the irregular rows of shacks, streets snaked and jogged, narrow and dusty. When the rains came, the streets became roaring rivers that washed away shanties and left deep gullies. Neighbours took in the homeless until materials could be salvaged and a new place propped up. Since it was impossible for a stranger to locate anyone without asking, Africans with passbook problems also found refuge from the police there. It was as if the very hardship of life in the Old Location created a great family in which each member looked out for every other.

In spite of the hardship, there was a strange contentment with Old Location life; in the midst of so much noise, a serenity. In the mornings women sang as they did the laundry by the water post and children played in the puddles left after the night's rain. Towards midday the sweltering heat drove people inside and the afternoon hours were quiet—even the chickens and goats sought refuge under the eaves. When the shadows again reached into the streets, women emerged to take down the washing from the lines strung zig-zag from house to house, and the children set out for the hills to bring back the daily load of firewood. Smoke from a thousand cooking fires collected in a bluegrey haze in the hour before sunset. Soon a clanging of pots and pans echoed from street to street. The first stars would be shining when the workers began to arrive home from town. They came in twos and threes from the city, slowly climbing the last hill before home, their shoes still caked with dried mud from the morning's walk to town. "They're here!" The word travelled several streets ahead of the men, followed by shrill children's voices and rapid little footsteps down the streets, then deep, muffled voices and laughter. Later came the noise of clattering plates and cutlery and of conversation as shadows moved back and forth behind the kerosene lamp in each doorway. Then, as the mist crept along the hillsides, the shadows became fewer; the lamps were brought inside, and quiet settled over the maze of dark shanties. This was the Old Location, as I came to know it.

Case Studies 3 and 4 below report in the people's own words why they did not want to move to Katutura.

CASE STUDY 3: From the Old Location to Katutura[11]

What is the meaning of the name?
Councillors Alfred Mungunda and Joshua Kamberipa called the township Katutura, which means "we do not have a permanent habitation." This name derives from the fact that since the whites came to our land, Katutura is the fifth location we have had to live in, in Windhoek. First, the blacks resided at the spot where the Grand Hotel today stands.[12] One of the people who lived there is Christoph Tjiteza, amongst others.

After that the second place where blacks resided was at the old non-white hospital, which today is where railway houses stand along the Okahandja Road.

Thirdly, the blacks were moved to the place where we find the Altersheim in Church Street, towards the south-west.

Fourthly, when the railway line was built to Keetmanshoop, most of the people were moved to the famous Old Location, with approximately one quarter of them still living in Klein Windhoek opposite the Roman Catholic Church.

After about fifty years of habitation at the Old Location, we were removed from there to make room for the present Hochland Park. We had been moved to Katutura, the great idea was that, according to the Odendaal plan, the Black residential area was supposed to be five miles away from the so-called white area, and Katutura was the desired distance from the town of Windhoek. The second fact was that the Old Location was situated on a very good, high hill that was the ideal layout for a luxurious white suburb.

Out of the hopelessness and dismay the two aforementioned councillors named the township Katutura because we had no permanent habitation since we were pushed around like furniture every now and then.

After fifty years of residence at the two mentioned locations in Klein Windhoek and the big Old Location, the government began with the preparations for moving the blacks to Katutura.

The mayor organized meetings and distributed leaflets in the locations, saying that the people must move to the new township. The government came to the people with arguments such as the Old Location is filthy and people were dying as a result, and they wanted to move the people to the new healthy location. The other reason they gave was that they wanted to develop the people and they could not do it while they were still in the Old Location.

The blacks asked to be developed there and they even put it to the government that if they thought the Old Location was filthy, why couldn't they clean the place while the people were still there?

The arguments went to and fro and eventually it became evident that the government had something behind the whole idea. As it became clear that the government wanted something else besides what they said, the people became determined in their efforts and they started to make the whole affair known even to the outside world for advice.

The municipal officials organized meetings in the Old Location but failed to convince the inhabitants, even with their threats. As a result of this last meeting the inhabitants decided unanimously to boycott all the municipal properties like buses, bioscopes, bars, etc. Eventually black women convened a meeting and took a decision to go to the administrator, to meet with him with the aim of discussing the grave situation in the Old Location, after the mayor had literally threatened the black people in the Location.

Mr Jaap Snyman, the mayor of Windhoek at that time, threatened the blacks that if they did not want to listen, they shall feel. The words of Jaap Snyman: "Bantoes, julle sal voel, wie nie wil hoor nie, sal voel."

What the mayor, Mr J. Snyman said, was true, because he promised us that we would feel and he truly let us feel on the eve of Thursday, December 10, 1959, when they shot at us and killed thirteen people and wounded more than a hundred. Eleven of these people were buried in one mass grave regardless of the fact that they belonged to different tribes. Until today, every year on December 10, we have commemorative services at the graveyard in the Old Location.

In our view the government murdered us just to deprive us of all our rights:

a) Prior to our removal from our second last location, where the Altersheim now stands, the assurance from the government was firm that the Old Location would be our permanent residence, but the people who had cattle in Windhoek were moved west to Okonjama (Khomas Hochland) and some were moved to Orumbo, and Otjihaenena, etc., because Windhoek was supposed to be a town and no farming could be allowed in the town or in the vicinity of the town.

Most people removed all their cattle to the above-mentioned farms, except people like Traugoth Handura, Heinrich Tjaseerue Hengari, Wilfred Kandjiriomuini, Christa Namuandi, Aletha Kaposao, Carolina Namupura, etc., who remained with a few cattle each on the western outskirts of the Old Location.

b) Since people could take ground according to their desire, they had big enough erven where they could do anything they wanted. People like Jarapuavi Mujetenga had a big garden where people could buy vegetables, etc. People could build a lot of those small houses according to their desires. I for instance had two, two-roomed houses myself. You could build houses for your families to retain your family ties as it pleased you.

c) Because you had your own ground you had to pay a small levy. I can remember that before we were forced to go to Katutura in 1968 I used to pay three shillings and sixpence (3/6), that is 35¢ a month.

d) Although we had one graveyard we dug our own graves, and as a result most of our families were buried almost on the same spot to retain the cohabitation even after death.

e) The old Location was near the town, with the result that the people simply walked to and from their work without using buses. At a later stage the Municipality started a bus service but that was primarily used by the old, sick, and the lazy people in the community.

f) The inhabitants of the Old Location were aware of the phrase about the black diamonds of SWA; they knew that the reference was not directed at karakul sheep but indirectly to the black population of SWA. They knew that they would be forced to travel by bus or taxi and to pay for that once they were in Katutura. They knew that in the Old Location they had their own houses and ground, in Katutura they would be forced to hire houses from the Municipality and pay a lot for them. Besides all these reasons, the principal one was the idea of being moved away because the Odendaal plan meant having the black families away from the so-called white areas.

CASE STUDY 4: Letter Written about the Forced Move[13]

Dear Editor,
Kindly allow us some space in your most honoured newspaper to publish an open letter to the Mayor of Windhoek.

With regard to a few reports in local newspapers concerning the shifting of the inhabitants of the Old Location to Katutura, we, the undersigned, wish to bring to the attention of the Mayor, and especially his council and the inhabitants of Windhoek in general, the following:

The refusal of the inhabitants of the Old Location to move is not just a "stupid, lunatical move by agitators" (as maintained by a few people who will not listen to logic or search for it).

There are definite reasons why we will not and shall not move. These reasons have been explained countless times to the people concerned with the movement of people (us) to Katutura, and therefore it is not " 'n gejaag na wind" (chasing the wind), to put it broadly. Still the need for explanation always arises when one reads all the trash which periodically appears in our newspapers.

We want to remain in the Old Location because it is more economical. The average cost of living in Katutura relative to the average wage is very high. While there are, as maintained, attempts being made to raise the standard of living of the primitive by giving them better housing facilities, there should also have been attempts to raise his wages to maintain the equilibrium between modern housing on the one side and the high costs which go with it, on the other side. It damages a person's self-respect if you today get a large brick-house as a present and you have to sit in it on paraffin-tins and fruit-crates because you are financially so exhausted that you cannot afford a decent chair or table. Therefore one would prefer to sit on a stone in your own tin-house with a free conscience, where you can console yourself with the knowledge that it is your own property .

The average annual income of a primitive married labourer is almost R200. Now to make a reasonable proposition. Will a person be able to exist on such a meagre amount if all the usual daily needs are taken into consideration? We now take Katutura as an example.

Annual expenditure of a common family:

House rental R48.80; bus costs for the whole family R35.00; food and other necessities (oil, wood, etc.) reckoned at R1.00 per day equals R365. Now there still remains clothing for the family, doctor expenses, travelling expenses during visits to family-members, etc., etc.

Will a person, however fortunate he may be, subsist on the above-mentioned annual salary? Definitely not. Therefore we prefer to stay in the Old Location where we are not troubled by the house rental and the bus fares. We would rather remain in the Old Location where a person can still say with pride—"There stands my own home, however ugly it may be."

The Old Location of Windhoek is almost as old as Windhoek itself. We have been living here in Windhoek for a long time and therefore we will not side with the people who scream: "The Old Location is a pest hole." "The Old Location spoils the appearance of Windhoek." "The people in the Old Location empty their refuse-bins in the street." The truth is that the municipality takes little trouble to see that the bathrooms (the taps in the bathrooms have not been functioning decently for fifteen years), toilets, streets, and other places, are kept clean. With the demolition of houses whose owners have moved to Katutura, the municipality just took the best materials and left the rest. Trees have been pushed over and the number of water taps has been reduced.

No person is being forced or intimidated to remain in the Old Location. Those who want to move to Katutura are already there. We who remain behind here, will stay here till the last drop of blood. WE WILL NOT MOVE.

Thank you for publishing the letter. On behalf of the different language groups,

> Headman Fritz Gariseb
> Thobias Akuenje
> Gustav Keister
> Fanuel Kambara
> Isaak Nariseb
> Noag Gariseb

A significant social and political rift developed between those who moved to Katutura and those who remained behind in the Old Location, as the Main Location was called after Katutura was built.

Those who moved were considered traitors by those who remained behind. This rift was especially strong within the Herero population.

Life in Katutura under Apartheid

The Katutura of 1968 consisted of about 4,000 rental houses organized into five ethnic group sections. People were required to live in Katutura in their own ethnic group section. In addition to the rental houses there was a single quarter area of dormitory-type housing estimated to accommodate about 1,000 people, and a walled compound located at the entrance to Katutura where Owambo men on migrant labor contracts were fed and housed.

Apartheid in South West Africa was enforced more rigidly than in South Africa. The small population and long distances between places made police control much more efficient than would ever have been possible in South Africa. Apartheid in South West Africa defined geographical, economic, and social boundaries between people. It emphasized distinctions between people, limited where they lived and worked, and influenced their movements and activities. Apartheid created heavy constraints on interaction between members of different racial groups. Marriage and sexual intercourse between whites and non-whites were forbidden by law. Separate entrances and service facilities for members of different racial groups were found in most government, administration, and municipal offices as well as many privately owned businesses. One local bank was popular with black and coloured people because they did not have separate service counters. Racial and ethnic categories were also emphasized by mass media. The only privately published newspapers were owned by whites; two in Afrikaans (*Die Suidwester* and *Die Suidwes-Afrikaner*), one in German (*Die Allgemeine Zeitung*), and the English *Windhoek Advertiser*. The South African government produced and sponsored monthly papers distributed free of charge to most ethnic groups in their own language and in Afrikaans for coloured people. The South African Broadcasting Corporation, the only public radio station permitted to broadcast in South West Africa and South Africa, maintained an office in Windhoek and had programs in various languages intended especially for racial and ethnic

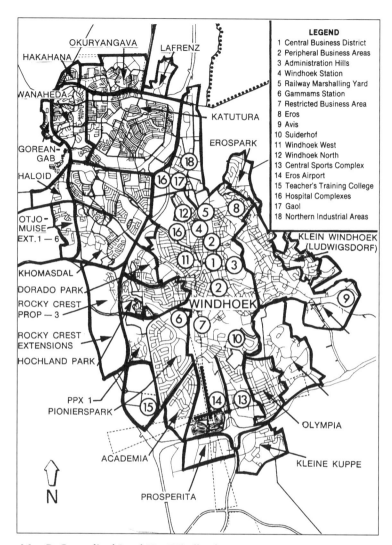

LEGEND
1 Central Business District
2 Peripheral Business Areas
3 Administration Hills
4 Windhoek Station
5 Railway Marshalling Yard
6 Gammams Station
7 Restricted Business Area
8 Eros
9 Avis
10 Suiderhof
11 Windhoek West
12 Windhoek North
13 Central Sports Complex
14 Eros Airport
15 Teacher's Training College
16 Hospital Complexes
17 Gaol
18 Northern Industrial Areas

Map B: Generalised Land Use, Windhoek 1993

groups. The most important apartheid policies are discussed under the following subheadings: urban geography, municipal government, regulations regarding blacks in the Windhoek area, and schools.

In 1968, the Windhoek Urban Area (hereafter called the Urban Area) was composed of three separate townships, each set aside for the exclusive use of one of the three racial groups: Katutura for blacks, Khomasdal for coloureds, and Windhoek for whites (see Map B). In this respect, the Urban Area was similar to other expatriate towns in Africa, with a small high-density African and, in this case, coloured area, and large low-density white residential areas. However, Windhoek was most similar to the apartheid cities of South Africa (Lemon 1991).

The central business district (CBD) was located along the main street, Kaiserstraße.[14] Most of Windhoek's service and distribution businesses were in this area, while most of the industrial and manufacturing companies were situated north and south of the CBD. The various suburbs where whites lived were spread throughout Windhoek: Academia, Pionierspark and Suiderhof are south of the CBD, while Klein Windhoek, Eros, and the prestige area of Luxury Hill are east of the CBD.

As previously stated, blacks were required to live in Katutura, where about 4,000 rental houses had been constructed by 1968. The only people exempted from this regulation were domestic servants who lived on their white employers' premises. In 1968, 1,138 Owambo contract workers and about 233 African women were allowed to live in servants' quarters in Windhoek (Windhoek Non-European Affairs Department Survey). For the remainder of the black population, transportation to work was expensive. Katutura was located about five kilometers from the center of Windhoek, and the majority of people traveled between Katutura and Windhoek by municipal bus for R0.15 a round trip, although some rode to work in African taxis (R0.20 a round trip), while others walked. Only a few Katutura residents could afford motor vehicles.

Besides accommodation, Katutura provided various other facilities. About ten shops were located in a central business area designated on Map C by an asterisk. Other shops were distributed throughout the location in the different ethnic sections, often operated by a resident of the ethnic section in which it was situated. Most people sent their children to these small shops to buy food everyday

1 Herero	7 Golgotha	13 Marula
2 Nama	8 Okuryangava	14 Bloedrivier
3 Damara	9 Hakahana	15 Grysblok/Vaalblok
4 Gemengde	10 Wanaheda	16 Freedom Square
5 Owambo	11 Soweto	17 Goreangab
6 Shandumbala	12 Luxury Hill	* Shopping Complex

Map C: Katutura

Note: Areas 1, 2, 3, 4 and 5 represent old Katutura. The above names and their bound-aries as indicated on the map are the generally-recognized names and boundaries within Katutura. This map is based on an earlier map of areas by the author, a map by C. Fröh-lich, and the municipal map of Katutura.

as the need arose and money was available. However, many people went to Windhoek on Friday afternoons and Saturday mornings, when they had received their paychecks, to buy at the large super-markets and white-owned clothing stores. Katutura also had a mu-nicipality-operated cinema that showed films once a week and served as a dance hall on weekends. Adjacent to the cinema, there was a small library. The municipality also operated a beerhall in Katutura. The following forty businesses owned and operated by non-whites were located in Katutura in 1970: general dealers (20), cafes (9), butcheries (2), barber shops (3), shoe repair shops (3), clothing store (1), gas station (1) and private dance hall (1).

Locally, most of the urban material culture was thought of as being of white origin, probably due to the white control of the economy. However, it was no more white than it was black or coloured. Just as baskets from Owambo and wood carvings from Kavango may be seen in white and coloured people's houses, they are also found in black people's houses. Many Herero still used gourds to store sour milk. Although some younger and more affluent residents had modern furniture, linoleum to cover the concrete floors, painted or finished walls and neat gardens, the general low level of income in Katutura created an overall uniformity of secondhand furniture of a low socioeconomic standard. Most people were reluctant to make improvements to houses such as installing ceilings or plastering walls, not only because of the cost involved, but also because the houses did not belong to them and they were not reimbursed for these improvements by the municipality, which had the power to evict them at virtually any time. Many decorated the walls of their houses with personal photographs and calendars, and Damara and Nama women sometimes put up sewn rectangular pieces of cloth with sayings in Nama and German.

Municipal Government

Under apartheid law, whites controlled all political affairs, including the municipal government of the Urban Area. They elected the mayor and members of the Town Council, while other officials such as the town clerk were appointed. In terms of municipal ordinances, the councillors and the town clerk were the officials primarily responsible for all three settlement areas. Furthermore, the administrator of South West Africa had extensive discretionary powers in municipal affairs. The municipality could approach the South West Africa administration and the South African government for consultancy services and funding for projects such as housing schemes.

In most areas of municipal government, Windhoek was independent and autonomous in decision making; the one major exception was black administration. All matters concerning blacks required the approval of the South African government's Department of Bantu Administration and Development. The Windhoek municipality had its own Non-European Affairs Department with a staff that administered Katutura and Khomasdal. The South African government had several offices that dealt with "bantu and coloured affairs." The staff of these various offices, the one municipal and the others South African, worked closely with each other, although they did not always agree.

The official policy of the municipality, which largely implemented South African government policy, was that blacks were in Windhoek only to work. When they were no longer able to work due to ill health, old age or for some other reason, they were required to leave and return to their previous home unless they had been classified as permanent urban residents. Even then, however, they were not safe from eviction, since old, unemployed people who depended on the municipality for accommodation and rations, had on occasion been required to relocate to a rural reserve (communal area).

One such occurrence took place in 1967, when all the old Damara people staying in the single-room accommodation in Katutura were taken to Okombahe in the "Damara Homeland." There is no firsthand information on the number of persons moved or the circumstances of their removal. Informants said two police trucks arrived, loaded the people and their belongings onto a truck, and took them away. The *Windhoek Advertiser* (December 10, 1971) reported that of seventy-two old unemployed people, all but twelve Herero had been relocated to reserves.

The only voice that blacks had in municipal government was through their township Advisory Board. These boards worked with the Town Council in an advisory capacity, and met with various representatives of the Town Council and the Non-European Affairs Department once a month. Board members informed the white officials of complaints and requests, and they, in turn, communicated them to the Town Council for consideration. The Katutura Advisory Board had no real economic or political power.

The all-male Katutura Advisory Board consisted of various white officials, one of whom served as chair, and representatives from the numerically largest ethnic groups. The Herero and Owambo were each represented by two members, and the Damara and Nama by one each. Three of the board members were supposed to be appointed by the white township superintendent, while the remaining three were to be elected by the Katutura population. However, no Advisory Board elections were ever held in Katutura. The board met once a month in a special chamber in the Katutura municipal offices; black board members wore special gowns of office. White officials sat on an elevated platform facing the black members, who were seated around a large curved table. Proceedings were in Afrikaans, which was translated into Herero. Not all members were able to express themselves adequately in Afrikaans, reflecting their lack of formal education and their age. On one occasion, when I attended a meeting with a Nama-speaking school teacher, the Nama board member took advantage of the school teacher's presence, and perhaps also mine, to make a speech in Nama which the school teacher translated for the embarrassed officials.

Topics frequently brought before the Katutura Board were problems with Owambo contract workers, the need for a better bus service and street lighting, the need for a market, complaints about the Police, housing matters, and matters pertaining to the operation of the board itself. A Herero board member raised a question about the Katutura liquor store at the meeting of January 25, 1968. He asked why a white was to be in charge, and was told that the job had been advertised and only a white had applied. The other board members had obviously never heard about the post. Frequently, matters brought up fell outside the competence of the board, such as vagrant children, allowing students who failed examinations a second chance, and low wages (minutes of Advisory Board meetings 1962–68). The fact that such issues were raised at board meetings indicates that Katutura residents had virtually no place to go to for help with such problems.

Apart from their official duties, board members also assisted individuals with their domestic problems, since there were no social workers in Katutura. When people approached white Katutura officials with such problems, they were frequently referred to their Advisory Board member. Since board members had a little influence with municipal and government officials, they were often able to help in matters concerning houses, passes and permits, as well as other problems. A woman whose husband died took her Advisory Board member to the bank with her in order to withdraw her late husband's money. She had no marriage certificate, but the board member's word validated her claim to the money.

The Katutura population showed little interest in the affairs of the board. This apathy was partly due to the failure on the part of board members to inform the people whom they were supposed to represent of what had transpired during meetings. An Owambo representative was the only one who called people together to discuss issues raised at Board meetings. Owing to the lack of newspaper or radio coverage, communication with Katutura residents proved especially difficult. Lack of interest was also a reflection of the fact that many considered the board to be nothing more than an extension of white authority, and people were therefore suspicious of its intentions, especially since board members received a monthly salary of R20 (20 percent of an average monthly salary) from the municipality. This suspicion increased when board members attempted to influence people to move to Katutura from the Main Location at the request of a white official. Board members complained that they had no influence over the people, and even claimed that they were afraid of being beaten up. One board member's house was burned down when he moved to Katutura in 1966 (Advisory Board minutes of October 22, 1966).

Younger people complained that the board members were all old men and would not "stand up" to the white officials. The average age of the six black members of the 1968 Board was sixty-one years, the oldest was seventy-five, and three members had served on the Board for more than twenty years; one had served for more than forty-four years. None of the six belonged to a political party or took part in any party's political activities, nor did they openly oppose government policy. White officials considered these board members to be model citizens and called them by their surnames, for example, Mr. Gariseb, instead of by their first names as was the usual practice. It was observed, however, that the Katutura officials also called them by their first names outside board meetings.

The young people's contention was borne out in October 1968, when a thirty-six-year-old Damara school teacher was appointed to the board. Shortly after his appointment, he also founded a political party, the People's Voice. He subsequently resigned from the board, or was forced to do so, and was later transferred to a small school outside the Urban Area by the Education Department.

As opposed to the Katutura Board, which had a white chair, the Khomasdal Advisory Board had a coloured chair. Coloured board members did not wear robes of office, and white and coloured board members sat around the same table during the meetings. Board members were also younger and better educated, the average age of the 1968 board being thirty-six. They represented some of the business elite of the community and were more politically active. Khomasdal board members also served without remuneration. At the meeting of August 1, 1968, a coloured board member requested that members receive a salary, complaining that board members received no salary and devoted a lot of time to board-related affairs. He was told by a white official that serving on the board was an honor, but that they could probably receive the same remuneration as black members, that is, R20 per month. The coloured man replied that he was ashamed at having raised the matter.

At the same meeting, another coloured board member complained that some people who had moved to Khomasdal from the Old Location were not really coloureds, that is, they were blacks. This was felt to be detrimental to the coloured people, and it was proposed that a committee consisting of two Advisory Board members and two Khomasdal residents be set up to decide suspicious cases. Among the criteria mentioned as relevant to coloured classification were parents' racial group, the people among whom the person had lived previously, skin color, and competence in Afrikaans or English. The proposal of this committee reflected the widening social gap between blacks and coloureds, and a change in patterns of interaction. It is also testimony to the fact that coloureds enjoyed a better standard of living as regards wages, quality of housing, treatment by whites, and that they were jealously guarding their privileges. Ironically, similar committees of whites passed judgement on coloured people who tried for reclassification as whites in order to enjoy their privileges.

Regulations about People in Town

Regulations affecting blacks in urban areas were defined in more than ninety-six acts of the South African Parliament (Lewis 1966:38), and they required an elaborate administrative apparatus to enforce them. The Windhoek municipality operated two offices that dealt with various aspects of black urban administration: a Housing Office in Katutura, and a Registration Office for passes and employment. A third office, maintained by the Department of Bantu Administration and Development, issued travel passes, conducted marriages and divorces, and handled Owambo contract labor matters and other affairs.

Movement into, out of, and within the Urban Area was controlled by the Windhoek Municipal Police and the South African Police. With the exception of Owambo contract workers and others from outside the police zone who required special permits, blacks were only allowed to enter the Windhoek area temporarily on visits. They could take up employment, if it was available, or come to town for other reasons such as to attend a court case. In order to travel legally, however, a black had to have a travel pass for each trip outside the place where he/she lived. Travel passes were routinely issued by the Department of Bantu Administration and Development, and a black had to show a travel pass before a train ticket could be purchased.

All persons older than sixteen years were required to report to the Registration Office within seventy-two hours of their arrival in the Windhoek area to obtain a permit allowing them to be in the area. They could apply for a visitor's permit and a permit to look for work. Although certain persons such as teachers, ministers, chiefs, headmen, and Reserve or Advisory Board members were exempt from these regulations, they had to have a permit of exemption.

When a black first reported to the Registration Office, he was classified under Section 10(1) of the Natives (Urban Areas) Proclamation of 1951 as either an *A, B, C,* or *D*. This classification system worked as follows:[15]

1. An *A* classification was held by permanent Katutura residents who were born in the Urban Area and had lived there without interruption. They could not easily be forced to leave the area, since there was no previous domicile to which they could return. About 29 percent (1,261) of the working black men were classified *A*.

2. A *B* classification qualified a person for permanent status on account of ten years' continuous employment with the same employer, or having worked continuously for different employers for

fifteen years. Only about one percent of the black men were classified *B*; from the records it would appear that many men who would in fact have qualified for this classification did not apply for it.

3. A *C* classification was given to the dependent of an *A* or *B*, but there were only two men in this category.

4. About 70 percent (3,040) of the men were classified as *D*. These men were granted permission to be in the Urban Area only while they were employed. If they lost their job, they either had to find a new job or leave the area and return to the place from which they had come. All Owambo contract workers were classified *D* and could thus never become *A, B,* or *C,* since they had to return to Owambo when their contracts expired.

From an administrative point of view, thus, a large percentage of men were only temporary residents, and this residence depended on their ability to keep a job. From Pendleton (1974:65, Table 11) it can be calculated that 41 percent of the black working men were actually born in Windhoek and would have qualified for an *A* classification. Many, however, failed to apply for an *A* classification because they did not understand how the system worked. Furthermore, it was generally felt that the classification system and other regulations were applied arbitrarily to their disadvantage, and that they were powerless to do anything about it. The strong authoritarian attitude of many white officials who dealt directly with blacks contributed to this feeling. I frequently witnessed officials shouting or speaking in a derogatory and insulting manner and threatening to call the police when dealing with blacks. As a result of the classification system, black urban unemployment was kept at a very low level. The system created insecurity and made the establishment of permanent ties difficult, especially since blacks in the Urban Area could not own land.

Although the passbook system in operation in South African was not applied to South West Africa, people were required to carry a number of documents, among them an employment contract or an exemption from carrying it, or a housing contract. Black women had to be able to produce a paper from the employer stating that they were employed, and a marriage certificate was always useful. All blacks were required to be out of Windhoek by 9:00 PM, unless they had a night pass from a white. If a police officer asked to see these papers and a black was unable to show them, he could be arrested, prosecuted, and eventually fined and/or jailed. If a black was not employed, had no service contract, or was not exempt from having one, he could be required to leave the Urban Area. According to the 1969 Annual Report of the City of Windhoek, 276 blacks were ordered out of the Urban Area, 75 households were raided in Katutura, and 4,961 blacks were cited for violation of some law or regulation, resulting in fines of R79,772 and 67,833 days in jail (pages 15–16 of the Non-European Affairs Report; see Table 1 for a full list of 1969 offenses). This was an incredibly heavy burden for a small poor population. The police raids on households were especially hard on the people, since they occurred in the early morning hours. Policemen would knock on doors and require all people in the house to produce permits and explain their presence. Those in the house illegally were arrested.

Katutura Administrative Regulations

Whites were not allowed to enter Katutura without a permit issued by the municipal authorities. These permits were usually issued for specific periods and primarily to businesses whose representatives needed to enter Katutura. Coloured people could visit Katutura without a permit, but they were required to have a visitor's permit to spend the night. Blacks not resident in Katutura required visitors' permits to stay in Katutura houses with friends or relatives. Blacks were not allowed to stay in white areas overnight unless they lived there as servants.

Katutura was divided into Damara, Herero, Nama, and Owambo ethnic sections for administrative purposes. The Nama section had much more significance in Katutura than in the Old Location. In the Old Location, Nama people lived in various sections other than their own, but in Katutura nearly all of them lived in a Nama section. Members of other ethnic groups, such as the Tswana and Shimbundu, lived in a mixed group section called the *gemengde* section.

The majority of blacks in each section belonged to the ethnic group assigned to that section. Only 4 percent of the 3,335 household heads in the Katutura Housing Card Survey belonged to an ethnic group different from that of the section in which they were living, while a mere 4 percent of the adults, taking into account total household composition, belonged to an ethnic group other than that of the household head. In most cases, persons living in a section other than their own were married or living together with a person of the other ethnic group. Ethnic segregation was greater in Katutura than in the Old Location due to the layout and more efficient organization of Katutura, which facilitated rigorous official control.

As ethnicity determined where most people lived in Katutura and created relatively tight geographical boundaries, people expected to be assigned housing on this basis, and the Katutura Housing Office operated under instructions that newcomers should be placed in the appropriate sections. There were no residential areas based on occupational or economic status, with the exception of one area occupied by black municipal police officers. About half the black municipal police officers, who were drawn from all ethnic groups, lived in the section not far from the police station in an area that later became known as the police camp. A police officer explained to me that this was a deliberate measure to ensure that the police would be available immediately in the event of an emergency. It was also the personal preference of the police themselves, since the black police were not popular with other location residents. They felt more comfortable living near other police officers.

When a couple applied for housing in Katutura, the municipal authorities assigned the couple to an ethnic section on the basis of the man's ethnic group. If a couple came from different ethnic groups and the woman refused to live in her partner's section, the authorities could allow the couple to live in the woman's section. As a result of the dominant pattern of the couple living in the husband's section, the children of these unions adopted the ethnic identity of their father, since most of the people they were in contact with and the children they played with belonged to the father's ethnic group.

A man qualified for a municipal house if he was classified either A or B. He also had to be the head of a household made up of himself and his wife (legally or traditionally married), or he had to prove that he had lived together with a woman for more than five years. Alternatively, he had to prove that he was the head of a household with a dependent such as his mother, father, other relatives, or his own children.

A man classified *D* was rarely allocated a house on first application. If he married a woman who already had a house, then he could succeed in having the house transferred in his name at a later stage. If he married a woman from outside the Urban Area, he had to wait for two or more years before he would be allocated a house and allowed to bring his wife to town. Men classified *D* often lived in the single quarters or as lodgers in a friend's or relative's house. Some men living in the single quarters had affairs with women who had houses, sometimes moved in with them, and lived together or got married. Until 1972, women were not classified, and an unmarried woman with children or other dependents was usually able to obtain a house. In 1972, however, working black women were required to register for the first time.

Schools

In line with the Bantu Education System of apartheid, the South West Africa Administration provided different primary schools for each ethnic group. If both parents belonged to the same ethnic group, the children had to attend the school established for that ethnic group. In Katutura, there were primary schools for the Damara, Herero, Nama, and Owambo, and these were located in the various ethnic group sections. People living in the mixed section sent their children to any school in Katutura. Otjiherero, Damara/Nama, and Oshiwambo languages were used in instruction, and the teachers were drawn from the appropriate ethnic group.[16] Afrikaans was taught as a second language, but was supposed to be the medium of instruction by the fifth school year. Separate primary schools for Afrikaner, English, and German students were located in Windhoek, and schools for coloured people were situated in Khomasdal. As a result of this policy, schoolchildren were more or less limited to making friends and playing only with members of their own racial and ethnic groups.

There were government and private secondary schools in Windhoek and in Khomasdal. The Augustineum, a high school located just outside the Urban Area, took pupils from the ninth to the thirteenth school year and offered teachers' training courses and technical training. Most Katutura students and black students from elsewhere in the territory attended this school. At one stage, there were plans to establish high schools in the reserves and to limit enrollment in the Augustineum to coloured students.

Based on figures provided by the Education Department and the Windhoek Survey, the number of primary school students in Urban Area schools in 1968 stood at 3,867 whites, 2,961 blacks and 1,354 coloureds. The number of high school students was 2,395 whites, 382 blacks, and 184 coloureds. These numbers clearly show the disparity between black and white education, reflected in both the number of students and the percentage of primary school students who proceeded to high school: 13 percent for blacks and 14 percent for coloureds, compared to 62 percent for whites. The percentage of black students is misleadingly high, since only about 15 percent of the black students at the Augustineum came from the Windhoek Area. Thus, only about 2 percent of Urban Area blacks went to secondary school.

This drop-out trend could already be observed in primary school. Most blacks left primary school without completing it. In 1968, there were 557 black students in Grade 1, and this number had dropped to 142 by Grade 8. Only about 25 percent of the students who started primary school reached the eighth school year.

In 1968, there were about ten blacks with university degrees in the whole of South West Africa, and about thirty-five blacks were studying at black universities in South Africa. The first black medical doctor graduated in 1974. By contrast, 241 Windhoek whites were studying at universities and colleges in 1968 (Windhoek Survey).

Life in Katutura After Apartheid— From Location to Suburb?

Changes in the Law

Is the Katutura of 1993 a location gradually becoming a suburb? By 1981, Windhoek had officially become an open city with apartheid legislation abolished (Simon 1991:178–9). Abolished legislation covered mixed marriages, interracial sex, separate amenities for racial groups, travel passes, night passes and the urban residence permit system described earlier. Blacks now own property and homes in the Windhoek and Katutura area, and people are no longer required to live in Katutura in ethnic sections.

Changes in Urban Geography

Much has changed in Katutura between 1968 and 1991. Between 1970 and 1980, additional housing was developed in six new areas of Katutura, which more than doubled the size of the township. Beginning in 1980, housing was added in three large undeveloped areas of Katutura, and this more than tripled the area originally available in 1968. Beginning in the 1980s, *erven* and houses in Katutura could be privately owned, and a variety of housing was developed, ranging from luxury homes to low-cost core houses. The compound for migrant workers was closed and demolished in 1987, and the compound residents found accommodation elsewhere in Katutura. Not everyone agreed with the destruction of the compound. When it was imploded, those present did not applaud. Pupils protested against the destruction, since they felt that the premises could have been used by the community. Evidently, the authorities decided to destroy the compound because it was so large and they did not think they would be able to "control" the activities that might take place inside the structure (Beining 1988:178).

Many previous compound residents found accommodation in Hakahana, which was developed on the northwestern edge of Katutura. Not all, however, found the conditions there to be better than they had been in the compound. Melber (1988:185–7), reporting on an interview published in *The Namibian Worker,* states that some workers found conditions in Hakahana to be even worse than in the old compound.

Some private minicompounds have since developed in Katutura, where several owners of small four-room houses rent rooms to migrants who eat in a common area, and a fence demarcates the boundaries of their compound; some rooms may accommodate four or even more men. The single quarters had become a large squatter community by 1991, and is still in existence in 1993. Several squatter communities had in fact developed in Katutura by 1993, with some squatters living in tents. Various new housing developments were under consideration for the future.

Changes in the urban geography of Katutura had already begun in the 1970s when Soweto was added to Katutura, the name being taken from the Soweto township in Johannesburg (see Map C). Soweto housing was rental municipal housing, much the same as in old Katutura. Following the abolition of apartheid legislation in the early 1980s, however, Katutura began to expand rather dramatically. New areas of Katutura, in which houses and *erven* could be purchased, were opened. The new areas virtually surrounded old Katutura, which local residents came to call the "old location." To the east, Shandumbala (more and more houses) was added adjacent to the old Owambo area; to the north Golgotha was developed; and Freedom Square, Grysblok (grey area), and Bloedrivier (blood river)[17] were constructed to the south. The Grysblok/Blood River area is also called Lubowski by some, after the assassinated SWAPO member Anton Lubowski. Luxury Hill (also called Rykmansdorp by some), where better housing was built on larger *erven*, was developed to the west. Luxury Hill was probably planned to attract more affluent members of the Katutura community who might otherwise have moved into Windhoek. When Luxury Hill was developed, the future status of South West Africa was still uncertain, and although apartheid had officially been abolished, the structures of apartheid were still very much in place. The urban planners were probably trying to keep black people in Katutura.

At the time Luxury Hill was developed for the more affluent, an area northwest of old Katutura was developed primarily for men forced to leave the old migrant labor compound; this area became known as Hakahana (Oshiwambo for "hurry up") and many Owambo men moved here.[18] The Hakahana area is characterized by many small houses with one or two rooms, a number of traditional huts built adjacent to the concrete block houses, and many *cuca* shops where food and drink may be purchased.[19] Housing in old Katutura and Soweto could now be purchased from the municipality, and some people availed themselves of this opportunity to own the *erven* and houses they had been occupying. In the mid-1980s, another area was developed to the west of Luxury Hill and Soweto. This became known as Wanaheda (an acronym for W̲ambo-N̲ama-H̲erero-D̲amara), and is itself almost as large as the old Katutura. For a while, it was also called Samora Machel after the first president of Mozambique, but that name did not last. The major area to be developed in the 1990s was Okuryangava to the north, also almost as large as the old Katutura, and Gorengava is being planned to the west of Wanaheda. In subsequent chapters of this book, in which information on life in Katutura is presented, one of the comparisons to be made will be between the areas of Katutura developed between 1950 and 1979 (called old Katutura), and those areas developed from the 1980s onward (new Katutura). Old Katutura developed during the apartheid years, while new Katutura developed after the repeal of apartheid legislation. The development of new areas in Katutura reflected the municipality's attempt to meet the demand for land and housing by new Katutura residents.

As if in continuation of the naming of Herero areas in the old Main Location after chiefs, the Herero area in old Katutura has become known as Maharero (after the Herero Chief Maharero), and some call Luxury Hill Meroro after a well-known Herero business/political leader.

Katutura's development has been primarily to the west and the north. There is still a buffer zone between Katutura and Khomasdal, a sort of no man's land where no housing has been constructed. This buffer zone does not effectively stop the movement of people between these two areas. However, the Western Bypass, constructed during the early 1980s, effectively guaranteed that Katutura would never become part of northwest Windhoek. The Western Bypass is a double-lane divided roadway, which was originally fenced, and separates the suburbs of northwest Windhoek (Windhoek West) from Katutura. Although the fence came down because so many people walked across the road between Katutura and Windhoek and it was apparently stolen twice, this roadway is an effective physical barrier between Katutura and Windhoek. The roadway has not prevented people from relocating from Khomasdal and Katutura to the various suburbs of Windhoek. Simon (1991:182–83) reported municipal data indicating that about 12 percent of former white areas had been occupied by blacks by 1985. Many coloured people have also moved to Windhoek suburbs and blacks have moved to Khomasdal.

One irony of Windhoek's postapartheid development is the integration of Hochland Park, the site of the old Main Location. Many low-cost houses have been built in this suburb and its western extensions, and many of these houses have been occupied by Namibian returnees. One returnee commented that she had lived in the Main Location before going into exile, and how strange it was to return to an integrated Hochland Park home not far from where she had once lived in the Main Location. Her present Hochland Park home is much nicer than her previous Main Location home.

Changes in Municipal Government

Katutura and Khomasdal are no longer administered as "locations" by the Windhoek municipality. In the recent 1992 local elections, Windhoek residents from all areas elected councillors to the municipality, and an Owambo businessman living in Katutura was elected mayor. Needless to say, advisory boards have not existed for over a decade.

Changes in Schools

On account of the growth of Katutura's population and the greater priority given to black education, the number and size of Katutura schools have increased. Katutura now has thirteen primary and seven secondary schools. "Bantu" education has been abolished, and Namibia is now orienting its educational system to conform to the Cambridge International Educational System. However, the problem of high dropout rates and nonattendance at school still features prominently. In a recent study of marginalized education in Namibia, LeBeau (1993:vii) found that about half the Namibian population will not receive any education beyond the primary level, about 65 percent of the schoolgoing population are undereducated for their age, and between 5 percent and 20 percent of school-age children stop attending school. Namibia now has a university situated in Windhoek, and the number of university students and graduates has increased dramatically since the apartheid years.

Changes in Facilities and Services

The Katutura of today has much more to offer residents than the Katutura of before. Another important difference is that black people are no longer restricted to facilities, amenities, and services in Katutura. Today, there are many community-based organizations that assist people with legal problems, domestic problems, skills training, arts activities, and small-business development, as well as women's groups, trade organizations, a Hawkers' Association, and trade unions.[20] Nongovernmental organizations (NGOs) are also actively involved in Katutura and Windhoek-based activities. The number of business enterprises operating in Katutura legally and illegally has increased dramatically. In Katutura today, there are 150 licensed business *erven*, the majority of which are small general dealers' shops, bottle stores, and other small businesses. As has already been mentioned, there are also numerous informal activities ranging from hawking to backyard mechanics. There are Ministry of Health clinics inside Katutura, and, at the entrance to Katutura, there is the large former nonwhite hospital which is no longer racially segregated, but almost exclusively treats black patients.

Case Study 5 below is the story of an Owambo migrant worker who describes both positive and negative features of life in Katutura as he experiences it.

CASE STUDY 5: Migrant Worker After Apartheid[21]

When I came to Windhoek from Owambo I first came on foot through Namutoni. Since 1959 I came on contracts over all those years. First I came on eighteen-month contracts, then on twelve-month contracts. In 1959 I stayed in the Ombongo Draai Hostel in town, later, after the Boers killed the Herero in the Old Location, I moved to the Hostel (Compound) in Katutura. I lived in Marula some time after 1979. The compound was closed in 1987 and I moved to the Katutura single quarters. If someone died in Owambo, then a letter would be sent through the labor office at Ondangwa. The boss would receive it and then I would be asked what had happened. But the white boss would not allow me to go to Owambo.

The whites used to give us little money and now it is better maybe after independence. At that time, we were asked for contract papers by the policemen and if I didn't have any contract paper, then I had to go to court and I had to pay for that and I would be sent back to Owambo.

I am married with five children and my family stays in Owambo. I don't have a house here in Katutura but I am living at my friend's place. My wife and children never visit me here because there is no place for them to stay. I go and visit my family in Owambo every year because I have to go and hear whether there are problems at home or not. I can also send someone whom I know to do it for me. I also send money to my home because my children go to school. When I go home, I find my wife at home without going on with other men while I am in Windhoek. The old-time wife doesn't go with other men while her husband is in Windhoek, but at the moment the younger generation is doing it. I don't know why but maybe it's because they went to school and stayed in the school hostel. It can be that they go out with their boyfriends because there are no parents at school. I used to tell my daughters that they have to get permission from me and my wife.

I have a problem with accommodation because there is no place where my wife can come and live. If I got a place where I could live my wife could come and live with me, but the only problem is that I don't get enough money for her to come.

Life is easier now than in the past. You can go to Owambo when you want. In the past, even for emergencies, you often could not go. Whites would say: "I bought you with my money and you can't go."

In the old times, each and every day we were asked to produce our contract papers for the police and if you didn't have them you could go to prison. The police used police dogs and if we did anything then we would be caught first by the police dogs and then put into the police van.

After independence, there are many changes because people are no longer asked for contracts or anything. No one asks why I am living here and why I don't have work. In the past, we were not allowed to stay with other people to make a group because it can be that we were making a political meeting. But now we are allowed to do it.

I left my wife in Owambo so that I could come and work. Then later I went back home to see her. I left all my things at home because there was no one who would come and even buy cattle from me. If I wanted to sell *mahango* then there was nobody to come and buy it because everybody had the same things. At that time those towns Oshakati and Ondangwa were not built except that there were only two buildings at Ondangwa. At the moment, those people who have cattle can sell them and get money. But for me I don't have even fifteen cattle. We were supposed to make a farm with our friends, but the problem is that nobody is going to do the work at the farm because we don't know how to do it. And we are not going to get money if we want to sell those cattle.

Despite the many changes in Katutura since 1968–70, dissatisfaction with life in Katutura was widespread during the 1980s. In 1986, a survey of Katutura sponsored by the Roman Catholic Church found many areas of discontent. A large percentage of respondents wanted open markets (80 percent) where they could purchase less expensive food; improved municipal services such as refuse removal, the provision of street lighting and playgrounds for their children (83 percent); larger houses that could accommodate extended families that would be more in line with African tradition (80 percent); more affordable housing (83 percent); and many were dissatisfied with existing health services. A high rate of unemployment (43 percent) and a large percentage of female-headed households (60 percent) were also reported (Garnier 1986:2, 3, 8, 14). Although the broad general findings from the Katutura Revisited survey project are probably representative, the methodology and implementation of the project had many problems. It is not possible to assess the representativeness of the households chosen, many questions are clearly biased, the data was not collected from a single informant but from a group of informants in the households selected, and the report itself is not objective. Nevertheless, the project was the first of its kind to be conducted in Katutura, and it was conducted under difficult circumstances with limited funding and support. The survey results do demonstrate that people in Katutura had complained about their living conditions prior to independence.

At the time that the Katutura Revisited project was completed, the future status of Namibia was still uncertain. Since independence, some of the complaints voiced have been addressed, such as the tarring of streets, the provision of more street lights, and more open markets. However, many problems remain, both as a legacy of the apartheid era and as a consequence of the new circumstances in which people live in Katutura today.

Notes

1. The discussion in this section does not include all communal areas in Namibia. There are many smaller areas such as Fransfontein, Otjimbingwe, and Ovitoto which are not discussed. Only major ethnic groups and selected features have been discussed in order to give the reader a general overview of Namibia.

2. The three largest contributors to the gross domestic product of Namibia in 1989 were: agriculture (including livestock farming) and fishing 11.3 percent, general government 9.8 percent, and mining and quarrying 9.1 percent (Sparks and Green 1992:74).

3. The Oorlam were a people of Khoikhoin ("Hottentot") and white—mostly Dutch—ancestry, had guns and horses, were notorious for their raids on other peoples, and were similar to the better known Griqua of South Africa.

4. Ridgway et al (1991:3) report documentation that the old Main Location existed before 1905. They also report the existence of ethnic areas, but they comment on the "fluid," loosely defined nature of the ethnic and racial areas of the old Main Location. One informant "described herself as 'coloured' and said that the 'coloureds' just lived anywhere" (Ridgway et al 1991:6). Another informant described how "Swahili, Rhodesian, Xhosa, Zulu, Nigerian and men from Tanganyika . . . were sent 'home' . . ." when the move to Katutura took place. The same informant commented that "we all lived like one big family. There was hardly any crime. One never heard of rape, assault, etc." (Ridgway et al 1991:7). The general tone of the descriptive part of this study is that the old Main Location was a community, and that resistance to the move to Katutura was virtually unanimous.

5. The twelve names I collected were: (1) *Otjikatjamuaha* (kraal of Maharero's father), (2) *Otjirukoro* (personal name), (3) *Ozombapa* (people with white animals—sheep), (4) *Onguatjindu* (name of an Owambo healer who came to cure people in this area), (5) *Otjitjaimba* (Chief Tjaimba), (6) *Otjikaoko* (place name of Kaokoveld after a man by the name of Kaoko), (7) *Otjirera* (a group of Herero people who used to soften the skins for Mungunda's people), (8) *Otjiseu* (Chief Seu), (9) *Omungambu* or *Otjimaruru* (place name of Omaruru), (10) *Otjikuaima* (Chief Kuaima), (11) *Ombandi* (the people of Ombandi, strong as a bull, who used to live in the Okahandja area), and (12) *Otjimungunda* (Chief Mungunda).

6. All currency is in Rand for the period discussed. For the period 1968–70, the exchange rate for the Rand was R1.00 to US $1.40. The exchange rate for 1991 was R2.85 to US $1.00. The steady decline of the Rand is evident from

these figures. Research for the book was completed prior to the introduction of the new Namibian currency, the Namibia Dollar, on September 15, 1993. I have used the former currency, the South African Rand, throughout this study in order to make comparisons easier.

7. The distinction between town and migrant Owambo people was rather important at the time. Those who were legally entitled to live in the location could not be forced to go back to Owambo if they lost their job, and they did not have to live in the labor compound. The distinction was reflected in the terms *kashuku* (a stranger at a place who does not know anything) and *ombuiti* (townspeople—foreigners to Owambo).

8. Ridgway et al (1991:29) report that no complete record of those injured exists, but a partial list of eleven dead and twenty-five injured is reported in their document. Their document provides the most complete account available to date of the events of December 10, 1959.

9. "Stayers" and "returnees" refer to the status of people during the twenty-three-year conflict between the South African Defence Force, Koevoet, their allies the South West Africa Territory Force, and PLAN, the military wing of SWAPO. This conflict, primarily along the border between Namibia and Angola, has become known as the Namibian War of Independence from South Africa. See Preston et al (1993) for a major recent study on returnees and stayers, and Tapscott and Mulongeni (1990).

10. Taken from the book *Battlefront Namibia* by John Ya-Otto (1981: 35–36).

11. Sondagh Kangueehi (Kangueehi 1986:29–31).

12. The Grand Hotel was purchased by the DTA and served as the party's headquarters, but was sold to the Kenyan diplomatic mission after the 1989 elections and is today known as "Kenya House."

13. Letter written to the *Windhoek Advertiser* on February 7, 1966.

14. Since independence, Kaiserstraße and Leutweinstraße have been renamed Independence Avenue and Robert Mugabe Avenue, respectively. Leutwein was a German military commander responsible for several campaigns against the Namibian people during the German colonial period. Some streets in Katutura with European names have also been given new names.

15. The Service Contract Survey is the source for the percentages given in this list.

16. Otjiherero and Oshiwambo are the Bantu languages of the Herero and Owambo, respectively.

17. This area is evidently called blood river because people have been killed in the area, and schoolchildren may easily be drowned when the river comes down in flood.

18. Perhaps so called because it was constructed so fast; it was also called Hainyeko after Tobias Hainyeko, the SWAPO military commander killed in a clash with South African security forces on the Zambezi River on May 18, 1967.

19. *Cuca* shop is the term widely used in Owambo for the numerous small shops in which beer, food, and sometimes other merchandise may be purchased. Such shops are found all over Owambo and the term *cuca* is derived

from the Portuguese word for beer. The Hakahana *cuca* shops are not the same sort of place as the *shebeens* found elsewhere in Katutura.

20. Community-based organizations include the Katutura Community Center, BRICKS, Council of Churches of Namibia, YWCA, Legal Aid and Community Advice Bureau, Namibian Women's Voice, Namibian National Students' Organization, and various community drama groups such as Platform 2000. This list is by no means exhaustive; it is only presented to provide an indication of the range of activities covered.

21. This case study is of an Owambo man in his fifties living in the single quarters in Katutura in March 1993.

View of the old Windhoek Main Location

Corrugated-iron houses in the Old Location

View into the Old Location

Traditional hut, though built from modern materials, next to a modern
rectangular house

Band of the Bantu Social Club

Furniture removed from a house in the Old Location prior to its demolition (1968)

Destroying the Old Location (1968)

4

The People in Katutura

THE CHARACTERISTICS OF Katutura people have changed over the last twenty years. The following discussion compares the people in Katutura before (1968–70) with now (1991–93). The chapter is divided into three sections: a demographic profile of Katutura people, a social/cultural profile of Katutura people, and a view of race relations outside Katutura. Gender, ethnicity/language, age, education, literacy, skills, occupation, employment characteristics, drinking behavior, women and children, and returnees will be discussed under the demographic profile, while the social/cultural profile will concentrate on social categories, ethnic categories, and stereotypes. The view of outside Katutura will focus on "race" relations.

Demographic Profile

The aim of this section is to provide the reader with an overview of the characteristics of the people who live in Katutura. Much of the data for Katutura now was obtained from the analysis of information collected during various projects that I directed or participated in over recent years (see chapter 2 for more details of the projects). The information on Katutura before comes from my previous research (1968–70).

Size, Gender, Age, and Ethnicity of the Katutura Population

The population of Katutura before consisted of people living in three types of dwellings: (1) Katutura houses (15,098), men living in the Katutura single quarters (895), and men in the contract labor compound (3,317). The total Katutura population before was about 19,310 people, and was 58 percent male and 42 percent female. The greater percentage of males was due to the presence of men (primarily Owambo) living in the single quarters and the compound who came to Windhoek to work. The resident Katutura population living in houses actually had more females (53 percent) than males (47 percent). Those aged fourteen years or younger made up 42 percent of the resident Katutura population. The ethnic composition of the resident Katutura population was Damara (41 percent), Herero (25 percent), Owambo (17 percent) and Nama (8 percent), while people from other ethnic groups accounted for 8 percent of the population.

The Katutura population now lives in many types of houses, the single quarters, and squatter communities. The 1991 Katutura population was calculated to be 91,464 people, which represents a population growth of 474 percent since 1968 (Table 2). Based on data from the 1991 Katutura survey, 53 percent are male and 47 percent are female (Table 3). The Katutura population is still overrepresented by males, but not to the same extent as previously. The larger percentage of males reflects the fact that more men than women have migrated and are still migrating to town. However, the Katutura population can no longer be viewed as part temporary migrants and part townspeople as defined under the apartheid system. The compound no longer exists, the single quarters no longer accommodate only single people, and people can enter and leave Katutura of their own free will. Thus, the resident Katutura population now has about 6 percent more males than females.

Those sixteen years of age and younger make up 34 percent of the population, reflecting a population that now has a smaller percentage of children.[1] The median age of the population is about twenty-three years. About 1.6 percent of the population is over sixty-five years of age. Thus, the Katutura population has a typical developing country pattern of a large dependent population (36 percent) (see Table 4).

The ethnic composition of Katutura now is Damara (19 percent), Herero (19 percent), Owambo (42 percent) and Nama (10 percent), while people from other ethnic groups make up 10 percent of the population (Table 5). The change in the ethnic composition of the Katutura population reflects the migration of Owambo people to Katutura. The increase from 17 percent to 42 percent is not as dramatic as it would appear to be. If the total Owambo population in Katutura before is included in the resident Katutura population, then the percentage of Owambo people in Katutura increases to 35 percent for the before period. There is no question that many Owambo people have come to Katutura, but they have been coming to Katutura for a long time. They now simply have more freedom of movement to come and bring their families if they so choose.[2] More details on the urbanization of the Katutura population will be found in chapter 6.

Education and Literacy

The educational level of the Katutura population before is not known. It can, however, be assumed that it was low due to the small percentage of blacks attending school, as has already been pointed out. For Katutura now, about 70 percent of the population aged sixteen years and older have eight years of education or less, with 10 percent reporting no education at all (Table 6).

A large percentage (77 percent) of the total population report being able to read and write, although the language of literacy was not specified (Table 7). Literacy for most is in Afrikaans or a vernacular language, but literacy in English will increase for those currently attending school. English is now the official national language in Namibia. Afrikaans was taught much more widely than English when Namibia was administered by the South African government, and the language is still much more widely understood than English.

Religion

Membership in an organized church was widespread in Katutura before, and it still is. Virtually all adults are affiliated with a church group.[3] About half the Katutura residents are Lutheran, about a quarter are Catholic, and the remainder belong to the Anglican, Methodist, Dutch Reformed, African Methodist Episcopal (AME), or the *Oruano* Church, while various evangelical sects are also represented.[4] Women attend church services more often than men. Those who say they never attend church services still reported affiliation with a church congregation.

The church provides support in times of crisis such as death, and performs important rituals such as marriage and baptism. With the exception of the Dutch Reformed Church, churches did not officially support apartheid in the past. In practice, however, the social situation separated people into different racial and ethnic groups. One informant, a Damara woman who was active in church work, expressed the situation in Katutura before aptly. Speaking about Owambo and Herero people, she said that "it is difficult to comment about them because they have different church congregations and groups." A history of mission activity among particular groups, as well as language considerations and separatist movements, created a situation that acknowledged *de facto* apartheid and, consequently, strengthened group boundaries. Church membership is no longer segregated, but language and residential factors work together to continue to maintain a sort of *de facto* segregation still today.

Work Status, Occupation, Skills, and Income

In Katutura before, men and women were employed primarily as unskilled workers. Men were messengers, made deliveries, did cleaning and general janitorial work, and they made the coffee and tea for their white employers. Women worked as domestic servants, and many earned money in the informal sector by selling beer and food. A few people had better jobs as semiskilled and skilled workers, clerks and salespeople. Salaries were low and people were dependent on their employers for extra food, used clothing, and other assistance in times of emergencies. Since older private-sector employees did not have any form of pension, some white employers would offer to buy the coffin for the deceased worker and provide transportation to the burial site when a death occurred. Employers often gave employees other types of assistance as well. It was part of the paternalism of the apartheid era, even though employers often gave that assistance willingly. The problem with this sort of assistance was that it had to be given by the employer rather than being considered as part of the conditions of employment. People often had to beg for it rather than expect it as part of their work contract. There were no labor unions in those days and employers could summarily dismiss workers from their jobs. The dependence that this type of employment created has not yet disappeared from the work situation in Windhoek and Katutura. Some workers depend on their employers, the government, SWAPO, the labor union or others rather than on their own initiative, and, as a result, expectations are not realized.

In the past, racial and ethnic categories played an important role at the workplace. First of all, there was a division of work on racial lines: whites had skilled, managerial, and supervisory jobs; some coloureds had semiskilled work; and blacks had primarily unskilled jobs. Further ethnic stereotypes could also be observed. Blacks preferred to work for Germans, saying they taught them how to do jobs, while Afrikaners often just wanted blacks to carry their tools. Blacks characterized Afrikaners and Germans as liking to be the *grootbaas* (the big boss) and acting in an authoritarian manner.

Many people in the country thought that there was some correlation between ethnicity and occupation. Often, white employers assigned jobs to blacks on the basis of their ethnic group, and members of particular ethnic groups sought certain jobs. Herero men were often employed as drivers or in other jobs related to motor vehicles and office work, while Damara men were frequently artisan assistants such as painters, carpenters, gardeners, or worked in butcheries. Town Owambo men had some semiskilled jobs such as stock clerks and shop assistants, but contract Owambo workers were almost exclusively laborers and domestic servants. Many African men worked as laborers in building construction, while coloureds were often employed as artisans, bricklayers, painters, and carpenters. Herero women normally only did washing and ironing, while women of other African ethnic groups did general domestic servant work.[5]

Paradoxically, the work status of the Katutura population now has both improved and declined. Reference Tables 8, 9, and 10 will show that just over half (58 percent) the adult population available for work is employed with a median monthly income of R500 (mean = R606, standard deviation = R543, n = 612, for those who reported working). About 35 percent are unemployed and cannot find work, and about 7 percent are not looking for work. There are more employment opportunities now, but at the same time there is considerable competition for jobs. Unskilled workers have limited chances of finding work. Owambo men sit on the street corners of Windhoek and wait for employers to offer them day work. Few have earned any money at the end of the day. Many of these men live in Hakahana, where three to five unemployed men share expenses and may even share a single room while they seek work in the city.[6] Of those who said they were unemployed in KAT1991, about half said they were unskilled. However, the remaining half indicated that they possess a diversity of skills, but they have not been able to find employment for those skills. The median number of months of unemployment is 12.

Compared with Katutura before, a large percentage of the Katutura adult population who would like to work is unable to find employment. This contrasts sharply with Katutura before, where most adults had full-time or part-time employment. On the other hand, those who are employed have a much more varied employment profile than in the past. About 10 percent have found professional employment; over 21 percent skilled employment; 32 percent unskilled employment; 23 percent are employed as clerks, civil servants, and in sales; and 15 percent work in the informal sector.

Thus, Katutura workers have gained access to much more varied formal-sector employment than before, reflecting greater opportunities and less discrimination than in the past. As opposed to an almost nonexistent informal sector in Katutura before, the Katutura informal sector is of considerable importance to household income today.

Many people now earn money informally in small-scale activities that they carry out with very little capital. They are unlicensed and not registered with the Receiver of Revenue. They work in five major areas in Katutura:

1. Street trading (including selling cooked food, alcoholic beverages, fruit and vegetables, and miscellaneous items such as clothes, cigarettes, and sweets).

2. Metal workers, backyard mechanics, other general repair activities and construction work, especially masons.
3. Taxi services.
4. *Shebeens.*
5. Various other homebased activities such as dressmaking, tailoring, and daycare for children (Frayne 1992:116–17).[7]

According to a recent study of the informal sector by Norval and Namoya (1992:25–34), those working in the informal sector are primarily rural migrants (the majority of whom are from Owambo), are about equally men and women, almost half report they work in the informal sector to survive, and almost half report they support between five and ten people with their earnings.

Drinking of Alcoholic Beverages and Other Health-Risk Behaviors

The brewing, selling, and drinking of alcoholic beverages has been a part of life in the Windhoek locations for a long time. Prior to 1967, the only alcoholic beverage that the indigenous African population could legally purchase or drink was beer. This beer was sold at the municipal beerhall in the Main Location that was built in 1936. The beerhall, a privately-owned dancehall, and many private houses where alcoholic beverages were sold (*shebeens*) were the most popular gathering places for location residents. Wagner (1951:269), describing the Main Location, mentions the popularity of !*kharib*[8] beer, the fact that many women brew !*kharib*, and that many people buy beer from the municipal beerhall. He also (1951:270) mentions that wine and brandy were often smuggled into the location. In 1967, the law in South West Africa was changed to allow nonwhites to buy all types of alcoholic beverages. The municipality attempted to maintain a monopoly on the brewing and selling of alcoholic beverages by operating a beerhall much the same as in virtually all locations in South Africa. However, it was an unsuccessful monopoly. The Katutura beerhall operated until 1985, when it was closed. The municipality evidently decided to get out of the beer-brewing business at more or less the same time it decided to get out of the housing business.

Shebeens were popular in 1968, and they are even more popular now. In Katutura before, the weekend was the most popular time for visiting *shebeens*. As will be described in more detail later, there were different types of *shebeens* and different places in the *shebeen* where people could drink, with some places reserved for more sophisticated customers. In Katutura now, *shebeens* are busy virtually every day, they all cater to the same type of clientele, and most customers are men. Afrikaans, Damara/Nama, Oshiwambo, and Otjiherero can be heard in the *shebeens* and sometimes—after a few beers have been consumed—even English. The most frequent topics of conversation include sports, social life, and women. Those wishing to enjoy their drink in a more sophisticated environment now have a considerably wider range of choices, such as the Katutura clubs or pubs in Windhoek. Many unemployed men spend their time at the *shebeens*. In many cases, women rely heavily on profits from the sale of !*kharib* and other beverages to support their families. Some *shebeens* basically operate as bottle stores with large stocks of alcoholic beverages.

The following Case Study describes *shebeens* as seen through the eyes of a white temporary Katutura resident.

CASE STUDY 6: Shebeens in Katutura[9]

Every street in Katutura had at least one shebeen where you could go to buy and drink alcohol. In days not so long past, it had been illegal for black people to buy and sell alcohol, so people had secretly brewed their own traditional beers and sold it to fellow township dwellers.

The white authorities had then woken up to the fact that money could be made from selling alcohol to black people, so the prohibition laws were relaxed and the municipalities opened beer halls in the townships. But it had remained illegal for people to buy and sell booze anywhere other than the beer halls, so the home-based shebeens continued to operate in secret, with many households dependent on the money they made from this illegal trade. It was, however, a risky business as shebeens were frequently raided by the police who would seize all the beer and money from the sales.

By the end of the '70s, the liquor laws were relaxed further and black people were able to obtain licenses to run bottle stores. But these licenses were hard to come by, and bottle store opening hours were restricted, so the demand for open-all-hours shebeens continued, and even increased, as the shebeens now also stocked commercial brands of liquor, beer and wine purchased in bulk from the bottle stores and wholesalers.

Shebeens had provided a far more relaxed, homely atmosphere in which to drink than the impersonal beer halls. Being so close to people's homes, shebeens were convenient too. At first, the police raids continued, but as time went on these became less and less frequent as the authorities realized their cause was lost, and white-owned breweries and liquor wholesalers profited from shebeen trade.

By 1988, Katutura's municipal beer hall had closed and shebeens in the township operated almost openly, although drink stocks were still kept well out of sight and new customers were vetted before serving them. Elim Street had two shebeens, the nearest —and our destination—being two houses away from where we lived.

Some indication of the frequency of drinking alcoholic beverages can be obtained from the information reported for heads of households in the HDL. About half of household heads report drinking alcoholic beverages (Table 11). Those who drink are about equally men and women, with some indication that people who drink have slightly less education. Religion has no influence on whether or not people drink. Bottled beer, the most popular beverage, is consumed by 22 percent of respondents between three and seven times per week, with home-brew second in popularity, being consumed between three and seven times per week by 15 percent of respondents. Wine and hard liquor are less popular (see Table 12). Pendleton (1990b:20) reports blacks say they have more problems associated with drinking than people in other groups. The HDL provides comparative data on drinking and smoking for the black, coloured, and white population of Windhoek. About half the black population report drinking, compared to about 80 percent of the white population. However, when the total amount of alcohol is calculated on the basis of all types of alcoholic beverages consumed, blacks drink almost three times more than whites. Thus, a smaller percentage of blacks drink, but those who drink consume substantially more than whites. As the level of education and income increases, the amount of alcohol consumed decreases. Statistically, the person who drinks the most in the Windhoek area is a black man with little education and income. Many black informants have commented that many people in Katutura drink to get drunk,[10] and the above data would seem to validate this observation. About 36 percent of the Katutura population report smoking in the HDL, and black men report more smoking symptoms than any other group in the study (Pendleton 1990b:54).

The risk of HIV infection (AIDS) and other sexually transmitted diseases is high in the black population. Liberal attitudes to sexual relationships and the failure to use condoms combine to put partners at risk. Those at greatest risk are younger people aged between eighteen and thirty. The level of HIV infection in the Katutura population is not known, but is thought to be increasing. For the country as a whole, the number of positive HIV-infected cases reported in 1989 was 129; the number reported in 1992 was 2,050. The central region, in which Windhoek is located, has shown a 70 percent increase in HIV infection between 1991 and 1992 (Titus and Goraseb 1993:2).[11] In Katjiuanjo et al (1993:29–56), over 90 percent of urban respondents (data includes Windhoek as well as other urban areas in Namibia) report knowing modern contraceptive methods, but less than 1 percent report the current use of condoms. About 15 percent of urban women report the use of the pill.

Women and Children

UNICEF's HHNS provides detailed information on the situation of women and children in Katutura.[12] Certain findings about women and children in Katutura are important to report. Infant mortality (under one year) is reported to be 47 per 1,000, which is the lowest rate for the three areas reported (Katutura, the Owambo rural north, and the Owambo peri-urban north). Immunization coverage of Katutura children is not as good as could have been expected in view of the greater accessibility to medical care in Katutura and Windhoek. For BCG and DPT vaccinations, it is better than it is in the rural north (Owambo), but the coverage for measles and polio is no better than in the north and is considered inadequate. Women in

Katutura breastfeed their babies for shorter periods of time and start solid foods sooner than in the rural north, reflecting a more urbanized lifestyle (Cogill and Kiugu 1990:xviii). Malnutrition was three times less common in Katutura than in the rural north. Undernutrition, stunting, and wasting are less common in Katutura than in the rural north. Better child nutrition is positively associated with education and income in Katutura and in Owambo. About 30 percent of the female respondents said they used some form of contraception (the rate in Owambo was 10 percent). The most frequently used types of contraception were injection (12 percent) and the pill (9 percent); condom use was not reported, but other studies report condom use as rare.

There are currently over thirty million "street children" in the world today. Results from research in southern Africa implicate urbanization, poverty, and family upheaval in the rapid growth of the street child population. Namibia is not exempt from the influence of these factors and the occurrence of street children. Even before independence, the presence of minor children living and begging on the streets of Windhoek, and other towns in Namibia, had been noted with increasing concern. The majority of Namibia's street children are male, black, between the ages of eleven and fourteen years old, and come from broken families. Some come from abusive families, some come from neglectful families, but most come from families that are simply poor. They come to the street where their prospects for obtaining food, clothing, and sometimes shelter are better than in Katutura. Most drop out of school and many participate in drinking, drug use, and sometimes prostitution. The government has a progressive policy for dealing with these children, but there are many children in extremely difficult circumstances, and many other social problems the new government must address. These children are, in part, the product of poor conditions within some sectors of the society. They are pushed out of the home and drawn to the streets by poverty, parental abuse and/or neglect. As long as there is poverty at home and opportunity on the streets, children will continue to go to town in search of a better life. The boy whose story is told in Case Study 7 is representative of these children.

CASE STUDY 7: A Boy Named Joseph[13]

His name was Joseph. He told me he was ten years old, but he had the body of a seven year old and the eyes of an aged man. When he looked at me that first time in June, I could not refuse him. "Misses," he said, "Please would you give me some money for food. My friends and I have nothing to sleep on but cardboard. Won't you pleeease help." I had heard all this before, of course, but I could not help looking at him. That is when I saw those eyes for the first time. "I would give him my spare change," I thought. "I will watch your car for you misses," he added as I handed him some coins.

He was like so many boys I had seen hanging out or begging in town, who offered to watch your car, push your trolley, or any other of an assortment of chores that would bring them a few cents. When I returned to my car the boy was still there. "I watched your car good for you misses," he proclaimed and put his hand out for more, as if he had just committed some heroic deed. "Well," I thought, "just a few more cents."

The next time I went to the parking lot, the boy was there. As I got out of my car, he caught my look with his. "I watch your car for you again, misses. I done a real good job for you before," he blurted out. As I handed him some change I asked, "What is your name?" "Joseph," was his reply. "And how old are you, Joseph?" I continued. "I'm ten years old, misses," he answered. "Well, Joseph, you don't really sleep on the street, now do you?" I probed. "Yes, misses. Yes I do." He had an audience. "Right up there, and there under that bridge when it rains," he pointed and carried on, "Would you like to see, would you misses?" "No, Joseph," I said, and hurried off.

Many times during those first few weeks in June, when the air thickens with cold, I parked in the parking lot, spoke to Joseph, and handed over my now expected contribution to his personal finances. I tried to go every day or so and always around two o'clock. During these weeks, Joseph had come to recognize my car and would run to it before the other boys. He would smile and greet me. I asked him several times not to call me "misses" but to call me by my name. He never did. I had begun to feel a distant familiarity with him.

One day I had been working elsewhere and could not get to the parking lot until late. As I drove in Joseph was waiting. I parked, greeted him, and made the usual arrangements for the "guarding " of my car. After carrying out my errands I returned to find him still in place. After the usual thank you and contribution, Joseph asked if I could give him a ride to Katutura. "You see," he said, "I am late and grandmother expected me long ago." "You told me you lived on the street and sleep on the cardboard with the other boys," I pointed out as I opened the passenger door to let him in. "Well, yes," he explained, "I do when I don't make it back to Katutura, but you didn't believe me anyway." As I drove Joseph past the other boys, who expressed approval by hooting and hollering, I asked Joseph to tell me about his grandmother and Katutura. "I live in the old part of Katutura, in my grandmother's house. She is very old and I don't like to go there because she has sores on her face and it's very cold and dirty. I go there to bring her food when I make enough money in town. Do you mind stopping at the store so I can get her some mealie meal?" he asked. He was a child of few words but the story showed clearly in his eyes. This was no child who used his money for candy and games; he supported his grandmother. I stopped and bought the mealie meal for him. When we arrived at his grandmother's house we said our goodbyes. I waited, but there was no invitation to come inside.

After that day I saw Joseph more often, asked after the health of his grandmother, which was never well, and increased the stipend. Now, requests for rides to Katutura came frequently. Many times as we rode through Katutura people waved and greeted Joseph. After I brought a blanket for his grandmother, he invited me into the house so his grandmother could thank me. As we entered the house the smell of decay was very strong. Joseph took the blanket and wrapped it around his grandmother and put the bag of mealie meal in a corner of the room that served as a kitchen. The house was an old "township" house that had neither electricity nor running water. Household items were scattered about and there was an open door that led to a small room with two metal framed, unmade beds. Joseph's grandmother was very old and clearly not in good health. She did not speak English but waved and pointed to the blanket. It was clear she could not take care of herself, not to mention a child.

As winter approached, I noticed that Joseph continued wearing his raggedy shorts and broken shoes. I wanted to take him to a low cost store, for warmer clothes, but he insisted on "clothes like the white boys," so off we went. He got the clothes he wanted and I brought him back to Katutura. "Joseph," I said, "I want to take you to a restaurant tomorrow for lunch, so please wear your new clothes." He nodded his head yes. I suppose I could have bought him a big bag of mealie meal instead of taking him to a restaurant, but I wanted him to have this experience. The next day as I drove to the usual place, I was surprised that Joseph had on his dirty, old clothes. I got out of the car and disappointedly asked, "Joseph, I thought we agreed that you would wear your new clothes so I could take you to the restaurant." He replied simply, "I can't work in those clothes."

I understood. "Let's go eat lunch anyway," I told him. As we walked to the restaurant I could tell Joseph was nervous, but I assured him it would be OK. Joseph ordered a juice, but continued to protest that he was not hungry. I could see from the look in his eyes that the prices on the menu intimidated him. I assured him that it was alright and told him he would still get "something" from me today as I knew I was sitting with the family breadwinner. Finally he settled on a large steak dinner. I had wanted to know more about Joseph and decided that this was a good time to try. "Where is your mother?" I asked. As he asked for another juice he explained, "My mother works on a farm in the south." "What about your father?" I continued to probe. "I don't know my father. I was told he was a farmworker who was fired by the boss." He had another juice, only ate a little of his meal, and asked for the rest to be taken home. As we left the restaurant and crossed the street to my car, the other boys circled around us and excitedly spoke to him in other languages. And then he gave the bag with his steak, which I had assumed would be his dinner, to the other boys. They grabbed the bag and went running away. Joseph was no doubt their hero that day; I know he was mine. We drove back to Katutura in silence.

The cold, long winter wore on, his grandmother's health got worse, and my research continued. I sometimes went out of town and did not see Joseph. Sometimes when I went to the parking lot Joseph was not there. But always when I saw him he was reservedly pleased. Many times I had wanted to hug him in greeting or goodbye but his manner and my conservatism prevented me from doing so. I had thought many times of how I could, no I would, "rescue" Joseph. I would take him home with me, no not possible. I would send him money every month, but to where? I would do something, of course. It was almost time for me to leave Namibia and go back home, but I had not seen Joseph in a while. I now looked for him more frequently. I drove to his grandmother's house, but no one was ever there. I asked the other boys about him, but they were all named Joseph or were at least willing to be called Joseph.

One day while I was negotiating with some Herero women for a piece of cloth I felt a tug on my sleeve and a thin voice say, "Misses, hello, misses. I want to speak to you, misses." I recognized the voice and looked up with the expectations of joy, a happy reunion of lost benefactor and patron. And then I saw his eyes, his beautiful eyes, clouded and milky. I pushed away from the women and moved toward Joseph. "Where have you been? What has happened to you?" I asked. "Misses, my grandmother is ill and is in hospital," he said, as though that explained everything. "But what has happened to your eyes?" I insisted. "I was in hospital too, my eyes have a disease the doctors cannot fix," he stated. "Maybe my doctors can help you, Joseph," I offered. "No misses, they say no doctors can help me. I think I must go back to the farm to be with my mother, misses. Will you help me?" I was stunned. "Yes Joseph, of course I will help you." That day we drove back to what had been his grandmother's house. We collected Joseph's belongings which included the brand new set of clothes and a familiar blanket. In virtual silence we drove to the Katutura bus ranks. We did not speak while we waited. When the bus for the Southern Communal Areas came I gave Joseph some money and waved goodbye. I never gave him that hug.

I wish I could tell you that the story of Joseph had a happy ending; I cannot. The prospects for an impoverished boy going blind from malnutrition are not good, and there are many "Josephs" in Katutura. When I returned to Namibia in 1991 I searched for Joseph, but never found him. However, my experience with Joseph led me to embark on a research project with a social worker. The research focused on the cyclical nature of street life, the push/pull factors that lead children like Joseph to the streets, and how they use their time, space, and personal networks to meet their daily basic needs.

Returnee Population

Just as some people decided to relocate to the communal areas when they were forced to leave the old Windhoek Main Location, some people decided to go into exile rather than continue to live in Namibia or Katutura under apartheid. An estimated 43,000

Namibians went into exile prior to independence in 1990 (Preston et al. 1993:5–6). Some of those who went into exile fought as SWAPO freedom fighters in the border war against South African forces and their South West African allies (South West Africa Territory Force and Koevoet), while others were nonmilitary exiles who studied or trained, or worked for Namibian independence in exile. Those who went into exile and came home became known as returnees, while those who remained in Namibia are called stayers. Reconciliation of returnees and stayers has been a national priority since independence. Some households comprise both stayers and returnees, making reconciliation more difficult for some than it is for others.[14]

Katutura and Windhoek were major destinations for many returnees. A survey conducted in 1992 found returnees (both military and non-military) in about 21 percent of Katutura households.[15] Katutura returnees are primarily Owambo people (87 percent) whose age corresponded more or less to that of the stayer population. Their level of literacy in English is much better than that of the stayer population, but the stayer population is more literate in Afrikaans. Fewer returnees are heads of households compared to stayers, indicating that returnees are generally living in the households of others.

Some returnees are better educated than stayers and received training and education the world over; many received their training/education in Angola, Zambia, eastern Europe, Russia, and Cuba as part of the support these countries gave to the African liberation struggle. At the time of the survey, 60 percent of the returnees interviewed were seeking work, compared to 28 percent of the stayer population. The employment profile of returnees differs substantially from that of stayers; returnees are employed in the military, professional, and technical fields in higher percentages than stayers. No returnee indicated that he/she did unskilled work, while 43 percent of stayers interviewed said they did. For those people who are employed, the returnee median income (R800 per month) is considerably higher than the median stayer income (R300) given in the WAP survey (median income from the Katutura 1991 survey is R500). It also comes as no surprise that returnee friendships include ex-PLAN fighters and many returnees; stayer friendships include a few returnees but mostly stayers.

Information on Heads of Households
and Their Spouses in Katutura Now

About three quarters of household heads in Katutura are men, and their median age is about forty years. Their ethnic/language profile is about the same as for the Katutura population in general, but they have received slightly more education and have a slightly higher literacy rate. The occupational profile of heads is similar to that of the adult population in general, except that a smaller percentage is unemployed. Almost 80 percent of the household heads and 50 percent of their spouses are working, reflecting the central importance of employment in maintaining a household.[16] The median personal income of household heads is R500 per month, and for spouses it is R313. The combined income of a head and spouse reaches the median household income of R800 for Katutura.

Social and Cultural Profile of Katutura People

People see themselves as similar to and different from those they live among. The basis for these similarities and differences are social, cultural, and economic criteria such as ethnicity, behavior and income. Groupings are also based on universal biological factors such as sex and age. In Katutura, people are continually grouping themselves and others according to criteria learned both unconsciously as part of socialization and consciously as part of coping and adapting to one's social world. The criteria and their meaning are part of the social and cultural world within which people play out the drama of their daily lives.

A person living in a large, heterogeneous urban community is continually brought into contact with people she/he does not know personally. Consciously or subconsciously, she/he categorizes these strangers, and her/his behavior toward these people is determined by this categorization. The complexity and implication of these categorizations depends on the particular situation and on the context within which the interaction takes place. This section discusses relevant categories based on similarities and differences between people in Katutura. The relationships between people belonging to the different categories are called categorical social relationships; these relationships are significant because they show the importance of many social boundaries, and they also act as a boundary-maintenance mechanism, that is, something that works to keep up a social boundary between people.

Categorical social relationships take place between people whose interaction is patterned according to some social category that is mutually recognized. Such categorical relationships occur in three different contexts. In the case of strangers who do not interact directly, it is a tacit acknowledgment of relevant social categories allowing people to divide a crowd of strangers into familiar categories. Such a process of classification allows the individual to impose some sort of order on situations made up of heterogeneous strangers. It is a common phenomenon of social life in general and urban situations in particular, where people from all sections of society are continually brought into contact with each other. Thus, a Damara woman walking down Independence Avenue in Katutura passes many people: some are also Damara, others belong to other black ethnic groups, some are old, some men, some may be friends. She will recognize the different groupings, and the way she would respond to members of the different categories—in expression or language—would depend on her categorization of them.

The interaction of strangers or near-strangers in public places such as a bar, on the street, or in a bus, is a second context of the categorical relationship. In these situations, the categories to which people belong may determine if they will talk to each other, ask directions, sit together, discuss the news or gossip. In a shop, the social category of the customer versus that of the clerk may determine how the customer will be treated and what language will be spoken.

The categorical relationship also applies to people who are not strangers. This third context of the categorical relationship involves people who have perhaps seen each other many times in the same shop, they may belong to the same club, or work together. However, although the people actually know each other, they may, due to the strength of categorical stereotypes, maintain social distance and prefer to keep the relationship at the categorical rather than personal level.

The Social Life

Social life in Katutura before was concentrated mainly on weekends, beginning on Friday night. There was little formality, and many activities centered around the *shebeens*. Apart from drinking, people often danced to recorded music. Many men had favorite *shebeens* where they could drink on credit, provided they settled their bill on payday. People preferred to stay close to home to drink; in the case of trouble or if they were drunk, they would not have far to go. It was generally said that if a man went too far from home, people were more likely to take advantage of him because he was a stranger. It was also dangerous to walk around Katutura alone, since robberies and stabbings occurred. The beerhall was also popular.

A *braaivleis* (barbecue), or simply a *braai*, was also a popular activity. A *braai* was primarily a means of making money. Either admission was charged at the door and you could eat and drink all you wanted, or you paid only for what you consumed. Usually, there was music and dancing. Recorded music was sometimes played outside a house to let everyone know that there was a *braai*. Anyone who could pay was usually welcome, and the crowd at these activities was sometimes ethnically mixed. Few men would take their wives or girlfriends to a *braai* or a drinking-place with them. In general, men and women went out alone or with friends of the same sex. Girlfriends and boyfriends often met at drinking-places, dances, and *braais*.

There were, however, many people who did not like to go to such events on account of the fights and quarrels that took place quite often. Many preferred to stay at home, visited friends or relatives, possibly listened to the radio or recorded music, and went to bed early. Life began early in Katutura; people would line up at the bus-stop early in the morning for the municipal buses that took them to their jobs in town. Katutura was a rather quiet place during daytime on a weekday.

Usually, there were dances at the cinema hall and a privately owned dancehall on Friday and Saturday nights. It was mainly young people who came to the dances, but older men and women could be seen there as well. The most popular music at such dances and other social activities proved to be recordings of African musicians and singers from Johannesburg or other parts of Africa, while American and English music was also popular. African bands sometimes played at the dances. Most young people and some older people preferred the modern dances, similar to the West African High-Life. Occasionally, however, older Damara and Nama people could be seen dancing the |gais (a traditional dance) and the ǂgae!āǂnāb (concertina dance music).

The social scene in Katutura now is considerably more varied. Katutura is no longer a quiet place. There is a hum of activity in the air, and many people can be seen walking about during the day or at night, on weekdays or weekends. Besides the *shebeens* and *braais*, there are also clubs and discos, and these are busy every day of the week. People also have home discos and invite their friends over for dancing and drinking. Occasionally, there are live concerts or political rallies at the Katutura Arena. Both Katutura cinemas are now out of business due to the establishment of video rentals and an increased concern for safety at night. Katutura today has much more crime than before. The Red Eye gang (perhaps so called because of the red eyes from *dagga* (marijuana) smoking) and *botsotsos* (criminals or thugs) keep people alert and suspicious. In the past, anonymity was rare because strangers stood out conspicuously, but the many town migrants and the greatly increased population makes anonymity easier today. Rapes, stabbings, robberies, and burglaries are quite common in Katutura. The Red Eye gang now seems to target only the affluent; previously anyone was a potential target.

Clubs and Associations

In Katutura before, the Herero had an exclusive ethnic association called the *Otjiserandu* (Red Band). The existence of this association not only reinforced Herero group solidarity, but also strengthened group boundaries. One of the functions of the organization was to serve as a burial society. If a member died, he or she was given a burial with all the local members of the association attending. In the case of financial trouble or an emergency, members would give financial aid or assistance.[17]

Associations based on the similarity of interests, to be expected among educated men and women or members of a common profession, were practically nonexistent in Katutura before. Businesspeople, ministers, or nurses did not have any associations or clubs. There were attempts to establish a boxing club and a students' association, but both failed to gain sufficient support. The only professional association was the South West African Teachers' Association, while the only cultural club was the South West African Educational, Social, Cultural Organization (SWAESCO); the latter only lasted for one and a half years.

Soccer clubs were by far the most popular type of club in Katutura in 1968. There were nine soccer clubs, each with a captain and about thirty members. All teams were affiliated with the South West Africa Native Football Association and paid annual dues. The four largest and best-known teams were the Tigers (an Owambo team founded in the 1930s), the Pirates (a Damara team founded in 1957), the African Stars (a Herero team founded in 1954), and the Orlando Pirates (a Damara team for newspaper vendors founded by a Zulu social worker in 1963 and named after a well-known soccer team in Soweto, Johannesburg).[18]

Club members usually belonged to the same ethnic group, and teams were therefore often called the Herero or the Owambo team. In most cases, they consisted of young men between eighteen and thirty who attended school together, and members were recruited to teams on the basis of their ethnic group. Every club had a women's netball team, the members of which were drawn from the same ethnic group as the men. During the season, there were soccer matches between Katutura teams in the sports stadium in the northern part of Katutura every weekend. The Football Association sponsored regional and national championships. Soccer matches were popular events and many people turned out to watch. There was also a tennis club.

Numerous clubs and associations exist in Katutura today. The *Otjiserandu* still meets; it remains the only ethnic association in Katutura. Soccer clubs are still the most popular sports clubs, and more than twenty local clubs now exist; local matches are occasionally televised. Netball, tennis, martial arts, and athletics are also popular. Also, many community-based organizations active in development, health, education and other areas are located in Katutura. Strauss (1986:35–39) discusses the activities of some of these organizations in the preindependence context. Furthermore, there are political parties, trade unions, savings clubs, and professional associations. Participation in and membership of clubs are no longer limited to residence in Katutura, and people who live in Katutura belong to clubs and associations that are located elsewhere.

Social Categories in Katutura

Many social categories based on the characteristics of age, sex, class, sophistication, elite status, townspeople, visitor, migrant, ethnicity, and race are found in Katutura, but these categories are not of equal importance. For any social category to be significant in categorical interaction, it must meet two criteria:

1. Cues must signal to which category a person or group of people belongs, and
2. Values and attitudes must be associated with the categories, indicating what kind of people they are.

The cues for differentiating men and women are quite unambiguous, and the roles for the two sexes are clearly differentiated. They do different types of work, primarily move in groups of people of the same sex, and usually do not sit together, for example, at church meetings. When a man's friends come to visit him, his wife will usually leave the room, and vice versa. On Saturdays, when many blacks go to Windhoek to shop in the large supermarkets or elsewhere, even married couples may separate to go with friends of the same sex. There are strong cultural attitudes about what is appropriate behavior for men and women.

These attitudes are still present today; they are, however, changing among younger people. Younger women are less likely to accept a secondary status than their mothers were. Women have more legal rights and employment opportunities today, which may also contribute to their more egalitarian status. Education and socioeconomic status also play their part in changing stereotyped male and female role behavior for some. The social lives of men and women are still separate, but not as separate as they were in the past.

Age is a significant factor, and most friends tend to be in the same age category. However, age does not necessarily denote leadership status. In Katutura before, many younger blacks did not accept the leadership of Advisory Board members because they were uneducated and not politically conscious, despite their mature age (the average age of the Advisory Board members was sixty-one). Older Africans, on the other hand, would rarely accept the advice of young men. They might admit they were better educated, but would not agree that they knew more. Today, there is more respect for education and training. Those who have matriculated (graduated from high school with twelve years of schooling), attended university, or received technical or professional training, will today be treated with a certain measure of respect on account of their accomplishment, regardless of their age.

In Katutura before, class stratification was not very marked. The distinction was essentially between the normal residents and an elite composed of such persons as teachers, businesspeople, ministers, nurses, and leaders of political parties. The elites were accorded privileged positions by others, and they were often distinguished by the way in which they dressed, the fact that they owned vehicles, and their housing. It may be recalled that Katutura businesspeople were the privileged few who were allowed to build or buy houses in Katutura before. The elites were divided into two divisions: a lower and an upper elite. The lower elite comprised primary school teachers, less successful businesspeople, some leading athletes, and evangelists. One important distinction between lower and upper elites was that the lower elites frequented *shebeens*, while the upper elites did not. Upper elites such as secondary school teachers, the two black school inspectors, leaders of black political parties and successful businesspeople possessed the important symbols of wealth and elite status such as cars and houses, and they usually kept aloof from the lower elites and the remainder of the black population. While elite status was of immense individual importance in Katutura before, it was overshadowed in nearly all categorical interaction by racial categories. As West (1971: 52–53) has suggested for one South African town, there was very little recognition of internal racial group stratification by members of other racial groups. The white population was not significantly aware of the elite status of many blacks; whites tended to treat all blacks alike.

In Katutura today, people who are more successful and have greater resources have more choices as to where they can go for entertainment. There are popular night clubs in Katutura (such as Club Thriller) which attract a multiracial crowd, as well as restaurants and clubs in Windhoek and Khomasdal which are open to all today. Where you go for entertainment today depends on your resources, and not on your racial group.

In Katutura before, sophistication related to elite and class status was often recognized categorically and frequently spoken about. For example, different categories of sophistication were observable at the *shebeens*. Those who could afford to drink bottled beer, brandy, or wine sat around a table in the sitting room; they were usually the lower elite. They were dressed well, knew modern dances, liked "township music" and usually did not get involved in fights. Behind the house, there were those who drank !*kharib* (home brew), often seated on the ground. A primary school teacher would sit in the front room in a chair with a bottle of beer, while others drank !*kharib* from tin cups in the backyard. In the old Windhoek Main Location, some people even built rooms onto their houses especially for drinking. One room would be reserved for sophisticated, well-dressed people, while a different room was provided for others. Today, *shebeens* no longer cater to sophisticated or better-off people, as these people have other places where they can go such as clubs in Katutura or Windhoek. Most of the conversation in *shebeens* centers around drinking, women, social life, and sports.

Unsophisticated manners and dress were often associated with people who were visitors to Katutura, that is, those who lived on farms or in the communal areas. In Katutura before, such people might be called *farm‖în* and *ovozofarama* (in Damara/Nama and Otjiherero, respectively) if they indeed behaved like unsophisticated rural people. These terms differentiated rural people from what the Damara/Nama called the *kai!ā‖în* (big city people), and they were also used to mark unsophisticated townspeople behavior. On one occasion, an informant made fun of one of his friends who had forgotten to put the lid back on the sugar bowl by calling him a *farm‖în*. Similarly, a young woman called a man a *kaffir* because he neglected to open the door for her. Attempts at sophistication in dress or manners deemed to be unnecessary were made fun of by the Herero expression *tate ngo owozondwa* (look at the one who is living in town like a civilized person) and, similarly, by the Nama expression |hû|hûsen (a derogatory expression for people trying to act like whites). The above terms and attitudes are still found in Katutura today.

Most blacks who lived in Katutura before considered themselves townspeople, even though many had little long-term security of residence in Katutura. No categorical distinctions between different categories of townspeople were found, although degrees of urban sophistication were pointed out. However, Owambo contract workers were not considered to be townspeople by others or by themselves.[19] They were migrant workers who lived in a compound that physically separated them from the townspeople, and they only took part in Katutura social life to a limited extent. For example, they did not go to the dances or the cinema. Migrants referred to themselves as *kashuku* (a stranger who does not know anything), while those who lived in the towns were called *ombuiti* (townspeople—foreigners to Owambo). Owambo contract workers had to return to Owambo and their wives and children when their contract expired, and just as Mayer (1961:99) and Wilson and Mafeje (1963:16) observed about the "Red" Xhosa migrants of South Africa, contract Owambo men usually got together in home boy groups. However, these home boy groups appeared to differ somewhat from those described by Mayer for East London, and Wilson and Mafeje for Langa, Cape Town. Rather than being groups of Owambo men recruited on the basis of similar rural-area residence, most were groups of men who shared a room or had met in the compound or at work, and the composition of the group seemed to change frequently. Two factors probably played a major part in the composition of these home boy groups. First, there are no villages as such in Owambo, and most people live in dispersed homesteads; second, the men were assigned to rooms on the basis of available space. These groups appeared to be a primarily urban phenomenon, although a kinsman or friend could be included if he happened to be in the compound at the same time. However, there were many men who did not like their kinsmen to know about their urban life.

Besides eating, drinking, talking, and singing together, many home boy groups went around Katutura together looking for beer;

they often caused trouble. They attempted to obtain beer from people without paying for it, and then started fights when refused. Most Katutura blacks tried to avoid contact with them. Home boy groups no longer exist in Katutura. Although Owambo men looking for work still come to Katutura and often live in male-centered households, they no longer move around Katutura in groups as they did in Katutura before.

Apart from the shops, the main place in Katutura to which the Owambo migrant workers went was the municipal beerhall. A few Damara women also frequented the beerhall and, in exchange for beer, taught the Owambo men to dance; some of these women became sexual partners of the Owambo men. Relationships between Owambo men and Katutura women were usually not of a permanent nature. If a contract worker married a local black woman, he had to take her to Owambo when his contract expired. Owambo men were unwilling to do this, since many already had wives in Owambo and few nonOwambo townswomen would be prepared to live in Owambo. Before the 1960s, it was possible for a contract Owambo worker to marry a local woman and remain in town "legally," and the origin of the town Owambo population was derived primarily from these people and their children. In Katutura before, Owambo contract workers remained "encapsulated" (Mayer 1961:90) in a social world that was oriented toward rural life in Owambo, primarily due to the influence of municipally enforced apartheid policies.

While categories based on age, sex, class, sophistication, elite status, visitor, and migrant did play a role in Katutura before, their importance was minimal compared to the significance of race and ethnicity. Categories based on race and ethnicity were very important for a large majority of the population. Also, the cues for and attitudes towards racial and ethnic groups were the best developed of all categories.

Ethnic Categories

In Katutura before, each ethnic category was distinguished by stereotyped attributes pertaining to physical appearance, dress, language usage, role behavior, gestures, and other characteristics.

Katutura residents knew these attributes well enough, so that few had any trouble identifying the racial or ethnic group of another person. The attributes described below were described by informants in informal discussions and questionnaires. Blacks in the Informant Sample of Katutura and about one hundred schoolchildren in Windhoek were asked: "When you see someone walking down the street, can you immediately see which ethnic/language group he/she belongs to?", and the people were also asked about "the most characteristic occupations" for men and women in the various language/ ethnic groups. Nearly all respondents said they could identify the group to which a person belonged, and proceeded to give detailed descriptions of attributes. The following discussion applies to both Katutura before and now.

In practice, one cue was not sufficient to allow categorization, and it was usually a combination of attributes that facilitated identification. Physical appearance included skin color, body type, hair type, and color. Most blacks have a dark brown or black complexion; the only important exception to this pattern are the Nama, who have a light brown to yellow complexion. Most Damara and Nama are shorter than coloured people, Herero, Owambo, and whites. Blacks and many coloured people have dark, curly hair, while whites and many coloured people have straight or wavy hair. Herero women are tall and slim, while some Nama women have steatopygia (large buttocks).

The style and color of clothing, as well as hairstyle and makeup may also indicate a racial and ethnic category. Herero and Owambo men often wore suits, white shirts, ties, and hats, and many took great pride in dressing well. Herero men would wear good clothes to work, then change into work clothes, again putting on their good clothes for the trip home. Damara and Nama men were less concerned about their appearance and would often wear their work clothes to and from work. Owambo contract workers could be identified by the fact that they usually wore blue jeans and sports shirts, although some wore suits on Sundays. Men dress less formally today than they did in the past. Formerly, wearing a suit was usually not related to a black man's occupation, but today many have professional jobs in both the private and the public sector and are therefore required to wear suits.

The ethnic group of black women was usually indicated by their distinctive dresses, which they generally began wearing during adolescence. Herero women wore a long, Victorian-style dress made from colorful cotton material with a turbanlike headscarf, usually made from the same material as the dress. Older Damara and Nama women also wore such long dresses, but they were made from material with different colors and different patterns. Younger Damara and Nama women often wore short, more modern dresses with crocheted caps or scarfs. It was often possible also to determine the ethnic group of children by the way they were dressed. Herero children, for example, wore a leather apron until they started school, and some continued to wear it during their first years of school. The style of clothing worn in Katutura today exhibits much more variability than it did in the past. Some women still wear the Victorian-style dresses, but many now wear modern clothing, especially if they are employed in the public or private sector. After independence, many blacks also adopted dress styles from elsewhere in Africa. It is not unusual to see men wearing West African-style togas and shirts, and women wearing West African-style dresses. Some women now make these dresses at home. Television commentators and Cabinet Ministers sometimes also appear in West African-style clothes. Television programs and music videos also provide role models for modern clothing styles. World fashion has increasingly shaped the tastes of all, and style and color of clothing are less racially and ethnically distinctive today than they were in the past.

Formerly, some groups practiced certain customs that created specific physical characteristics. Some Herero and Owambo extracted their lower incisor teeth, some Damara used to cut off the tip of their little finger, and Owambo women were given two vertical marks on both cheeks. Most of these customs, which were often connected with initiation rites, are no longer practiced today. The Herero were the only black ethnic group in South West Africa to practice circumcision. While there were a few Herero from the communal areas who performed the operation, many preferred to take their sons to the hospital, where the operation was performed by a medical doctor.

Stereotypes for Other Ethnic Groups

Blacks of one ethnic group had a variety of terms and attitudes for members of other ethnic groups. Terms such as Herero or Nama exist in most languages, often in a slightly modified form to conform to the grammar and phonology of the speaker's language, for example, the Nama term for Herero was *Hereron*, although more descriptive terms were often used. The Herero were identified by all other ethnic groups as being very proud and arrogant. This attitude was reflected in the Herero term *ovatwa*, which was used for all non-Herero and means, in a derogatory sense, a non-Herero person with a low status; the Owambo were the only people who were not *ovatwa*. Herero called Damara *ovazorotwa* (black strangers). This term and others reflect the fact that the Herero had little respect for the Damara. Herero terms for the Nama and Owambo were more neutral, and whites were called *ovirumbu* (yellow things). The pride and arrogance of Herero women was remarked on by many informants who said it could be seen in the way they walked—always slow, never running, even if it meant missing the bus—and the Herero women's reluctance to speak other languages.

The Nama also had an abusive term for the Damara, calling them *Xaudaman* (excrement people), although Damara were heard using this term jokingly for themselves (see Table 13 for ethnic group terms). The Owambo were called |*Napen* (swingers), which had a derogatory connotation. Nama and Damara called Afrikaners |*Khoran* (rough people) and Germans !*Omkhoen* (pollards—trees cut back to the trunk). The Nama called all whites collectively |*Hûn*. A proposal in the 1960s to place the Nama under the Department of Coloured Affairs was thought at the time to possibly have far-reaching effects on the other black groups' image of the Nama, especially if they were moved to Khomasdal. The official explanation for the reclassification of the Nama to the coloured category was that the Nama were more like coloured people than blacks. Their light complexion was undoubtedly the reason for the proposed reclassification. However, the Nama were not moved to Khomasdal, and they were not required to attend coloured schools as part of apartheid education.

The Damara had a reputation for being friendly, ready to laugh, and easy to make friends with. Damara informants mentioned having a feeling of inferiority because the Herero and Nama looked down on them as "their former slaves." Some Damara also lamented the fact that the Nama said that they had lost their own language and taken over that of the Nama, but there was nevertheless also a joking relationship between the Nama and Damara. Members of other ethnic groups said that the Damara were "dirty" and their women "loose." It probably did not help the reputation of Damara women that many younger women wore miniskirts, slacksuits, wigs, and lipstick.

Members of other ethnic groups considered the Owambo to be hard to make friends with, but lifelong friends once a friendship had been established. A certain amount of community spirit existed among the Owambo, which is also reflected by the fact that they were the only ethnic group from which members would gather to hear reports from their Advisory Board members. Town Owambo were generally thought of well by blacks from other ethnic groups, and they were clearly distinguished—by themselves and others—from the migrant Owambo contract workers, who were considered to be troublemakers.

The importance of all the terms, attitudes, and cues described above for racial and ethnic groups was that they allowed individuals of one group to refer terminologically and descriptively to other groups that were meaningfully differentiated in Katutura and Windhoek. Either a particular language was associated with an ethnic category, or a different variety of the same language was spoken. The home languages associated with each ethnic category were Afrikaans (closely related to Dutch)—spoken by the Afrikaner and coloured people; English—spoken by the English; German—spoken by Germans; Otjiherero (a Bantu language[20])—spoken by the Herero; Nama (non-Bantu click language)—spoken by the Damara and Nama; and Oshiwambo (there are seven closely related Oshiwambo languages that belong to the Bantu language family)—spoken by the Owambo. There are different varieties of all the above languages, for example, the German spoken locally was often called *Südwesterdeutsch* and contains many words borrowed from African languages. Communication between members of these different ethnic groups, if they did not speak the same language, usually took place in

Afrikaans. Afrikaans was the *lingua franca* in the Windhoek area; it was taught in the schools and most whites used it when speaking to blacks. Afrikaners expected Africans to speak Afrikaans to them and became annoyed if a Herero or a coloured, for example, spoke English. English and German people also expected to speak Afrikaans to Africans and coloureds, but would usually speak English or German if the black or coloured person preferred it. However, whites used different varieties or alternate ways of speaking German, and to a lesser extent Afrikaans and English, when speaking to black and coloured people.

These simplified varieties of languages were undoubtedly pidgin forms of the languages concerned, with simplified grammar and alternate vocabulary choices. Although whites asserted that these simplifications facilitated communication, they also served another function. They created a different variety of the language, which emphasized the difference between blacks and whites, that is, whites used one variety when speaking among themselves, and another when speaking to blacks. Older blacks usually had a speaking knowledge of German, but that language was seldom used between blacks. A few blacks spoke English and its use carried some prestige, especially among the Herero, Owambo, and Damara. Loan words from other languages were frequently used by members of all groups. Köhler (1960:339–41), for example, lists about 450 loan words used by Windhoek Herero. Many loan words were also found in Nama, Afrikaans, and English.

English is increasingly spoken today, since it is the official language in Namibia and has replaced Afrikaans as the medium of instruction after the initial phase of mother-tongue instruction in the schools. However, English is not widely understood by the black population of Katutura, and even less so by people living elsewhere in Namibia. A 1992 consultancy report prepared by myself and LeBeau (Pendleton and LeBeau 1992) found that most Namibian radio listeners wanted radio programs in their own vernacular and that the level of English comprehension was low. The report recommended that English be introduced on the various indigenous language services of the Namibian Broadcasting Corporation in order to familiarize listeners with the sound and vocabulary of English.[21]

As part of the 1988 HDL, the two questions previously mentioned about ethnic identity from the 1968 fieldwork were included in the questionnaire, as was a general question about "how well members of different language/ethnic groups get along in Namibia today." LeBeau (1991) did a detailed analysis of the answers to these three open-ended questions for the 570 respondents, 301 of which were Katutura residents. For the people living in Katutura, she found that about 85 percent said they could determine a person's ethnicity by seeing her/him walk down the street. The attributes most used in identification are clothes, complexion, and physical appearance. However, she found that behavior and attitude ranked higher than overt physical cues, and she concluded that these behavior/attitude characteristics were ethnic stereotypes. People readily gave these nonobservational behavioral/attitudinal stereotypes as part of the characteristics they identified when seeing people walk down the street. The least favorable stereotypes are those for the Damara and Afrikaners, the least unfavorable are for the Herero and English, while the Nama, Owambo, German, and coloured ethnic groups lie in the middle (LeBeau 1991:40). Two interesting results were found for the analysis of ethnic and gender patterns for occupation. The analysis found that respondents believe that individuals from each gender and ethnic group typically have a limited number of occupations, that is, ethnic/gender occupational stereotyping is widespread. Occupational stereotypes for women are the strongest (LeBeau 1991:49). The third question about general interaction between members of various ethnic groups revealed that respondents are most concerned about discrimination, racism, and the government. Perhaps the most interesting finding from LeBeau's study is that variables correlated with the racial group of the respondent (residence location, income, religion, education, occupation, and marriage attitudes) are highly correlated to the stereotypes given, while variables not correlated with racial group (such as age, gender, marital status, spouse's ethnicity, and way of life) are not significant when analyzed by the stereotypes. She concludes that "the stereotypes given are learned through the respondent's group, are firmly held regardless of the respondent's demographic features, and are widespread throughout the society" (LeBeau 1991:71). This survey was conducted prior to Namibia's independence, but indicates that the strength of ethnic stereotyping has not changed much since 1968.

The View From Katutura— Race Relations Outside Katutura

Value orientations and attitudes, frequently reflected in language usage patterns and ethnic and racial group terms, were associated with the various racial and ethnic categories in 1968. It must be emphasized that not all members of each group held the following attitudes or beliefs, but they were widespread and representative. Whites thought blacks were unreliable, irresponsible, and would steal when given the chance. They were considered less "developed" than whites, and most whites thought it would take at least a generation and some thought a century or more for blacks to reach the stage of white civilization.

These views were shared by Germans, Afrikaners, and English and were reflected in the frequent use of the derogatory term for Africans —kaffir—often preceded by a descriptive adjective for emphasis. These attitudes were frequently expressed as rationalizations for the white dominance of the society. Whites who contradicted these attitudes were often labeled as communists or liberals; such people were called *kafferboetie* (little kaffir brother) in Afrikaans. One white who frequently criticized these attitudes was accused of having black or coloured blood.[22] Such attitudes still exist today, but are expressed less frequently.

Categorical Relationships: Blacks and Whites

During the apartheid years, the superordinate position of whites and the subordinate position of blacks, and to a slightly less extent coloureds, were reflected in categorical relationships between these groups. Black/white relationships were marked by inequality and paternalism, as has been discussed earlier. Language usage played an important part, with linguistic role markers used to indicate the difference in status. Blacks and coloureds called white men mister, master, and *baas* (boss), sometimes followed by the white's surname or first name; white women were called *miesies*; older whites were referred to as *oubaas*, while younger whites were called *kleinbaas* and *kleinmiesies* and *basie*. Whites called blacks and coloureds by their first name. When speaking to blacks, Germans used the familiar *du* (you), which would be rude if used in a categorical relationship with another German. Only in certain situations, for example, when speaking with a black church minister, would an Afrikaner allow a black to call him *Meneer* (Mister). *Meneer* was primarily used only between whites or only between coloured people. Today, many people address each other according to nonracial categories such as employment status, and whites may be heard saying Sir (or *Meneer*) to a black and vice versa without it having a racial overtone. People are more polite and more respectful to each other today, which stands in marked contrast to the embarrassment and humiliation that interaction between black and white people often exhibited in the past.

Social distance during the apartheid years was also marked by other customs. Whites, blacks, and coloureds did not normally eat or drink together. There was hardly an exception made to this rule. In shops, where blacks made the tea and coffee, the whites took theirs together; blacks usually sat in the back of the store or went outside to have theirs. Whites and nonwhites usually had separate working areas that kept them separated during much of the work situation. White-owned clothing stores in Windhoek did not normally allow nonwhites to try on clothes prior to purchase. There were few formal occasions on which whites, blacks, and coloureds came together. At the few occasions when they actually did, such as sports contests at which nonwhites were allowed as spectators, they were still segregated spatially and given differential treatment. Informal social mixing between whites and nonwhites was not practiced. Many businesses and municipal, government, and administration offices had separate facilities and counters, and marriage and sexual intercourse between whites and nonwhites were forbidden by law. Today, such racist practices are no longer found and are against the law, and mixed marriages are not uncommon.

If whites and nonwhites were going to shake hands during the apartheid years, which seldom happened, the white extended his hand first. Blacks and coloureds would never put their hands out first, since they might be refused. When nonwhites rode in cars and trucks with whites, they usually sat by themselves in the back seat of the car. There was even a particular way of offering a cigarette to a black. Whites took the cigarette out of the box and gave it to the black. There were individual exceptions to these customs, but they were the dominant pattern in Windhoek. Whites who treated blacks differently were viewed with suspicion. A white car salesman related how he had observed a white behaving strangely; the man offered blacks cigarettes out of the box and let them ride in front with him. He said the white was arrested by the police, although he could not say why. He suspected the white might have been a United Nations spy. This example indicated how closely other whites' behavior was watched by whites, but it was also watched by blacks.

Race relations have changed considerably over the last ten years, and continue to change since independence. A national policy of racial and wartime reconciliation is in force, and racist behavior is viewed as unacceptable and illegal today. A prominent white was brought to court for refusing to serve a black government official. Windhoek has experienced the most pronounced changes in race relations. Elsewhere in the country, the changes are not as noticeable— the more remote the place, the less change has taken place, especially in the commercial farming areas. Overt racial discrimination is rarely seen in Windhoek; indeed, it is illegal, and acts of public discrimination would be prosecuted in the courts if reported. It is rare to hear the derogatory term kaffir used in Windhoek, and the Afrikaans *Meneer* (Mister) is now used without racial overtones. Social distance between black and coloured people has also declined. However, social distance between blacks and whites is still considerable, promoted in part by the fact that most residential areas in Windhoek are still *de facto* racially segregated. Only a few areas such as Windhoek West have become partially integrated. Renting or buying a house in a Windhoek suburb requires a job and money, something that many blacks do not have. Those who have integrated are primarily middle class or better. None of the black members of the cabinet live in Katutura.

Considerable integration has occurred in employment, especially in the public sector, and affirmative action programs are implemented to encourage black employment. Coloured and black employees are seen all over Windhoek today, in marked contrast to twenty years ago. Shaking hands, polite greeting, and social interaction based on equality is at least overtly widespread. Integrated groups at Katutura discos and Windhoek restaurants are a common sight. Since most public figures, from cabinet ministers to the mayor of Windhoek, are blacks, the image of blacks and coloured people in positions of leadership stands in marked contrast to the past. The Namibian Broadcasting Corporation presents television and radio programs aimed at promoting public awareness of social equality. Windhoek newspapers, especially the *Namibian,* are quick to report alleged cases of racism and discrimination.

Notes

1. Cogill and Kiugu (1990:16) report that 50 percent is the usual percentage in rural areas.

2. Wagner (1951:96) reports that the Owambo/Kavango population in the Windhoek urban area in 1950 was 25 percent of the black population and 13 percent of the population in the Windhoek Main Location. It can be assumed that the Owambo/Kavango population comprised primarily Owambo.

3. Wagner (1951:239) reports that 86 percent of the non-European population of the Windhoek district (rural and urban) were registered church members, and he comments that church membership was probably higher for urban dwellers. The high church membership is related to mission activity in the past as well as today. Data on religion for Katutura now comes from the HDL Survey.

4. The Nama were the first to break with the Lutherans. In 1946 some left the Lutheran Church and affiliated themselves with the AME. They feared a threatened merger with the NGK, and also desired more autonomy and leadership opportunities. The AME had a church building in the Old Location, and they plan to build a church in Katutura. Although the AME minister is a Herero, the approximately 200 members are mostly Nama. The Katutura AME is not an independent church, since it is affiliated with a larger church group in South Africa and America, but the Herero *Oruano* Church is independent.

In 1955 some Herero formed an independent church, the *Okereka Jevangeli Joruwano* (the Protestant Unity Church), widely known as the *Oruano* (unity) Church (Kandovazu 1968:16–24). The breakaway from the Lutherans was due to a lack of leadership opportunities and doubts about what their church contributions were being used for, disapproval of the fact that the Lutheran missionary Dr. H. Vedder had been appointed a Senator in the South African Parliament, and a general revolt against the race policies of the Lutheran Church and the mission society in general.

The *Oruano* is an Ethiopian-type separatist church (Sundkler 1961) that retained much in common with the Lutherans, although no mission-trained pastors were allowed to join. Membership is only open to Herero, and much secrecy surrounds meetings. One *Oruano* preacher said the services were similar to those of the Lutheran Church. The original *Oruano* Church met in the Old Location in the Red Band Association hall. The original church has split into four different groups, some of which are led by prophets (Kandovazu 1968:27–29). One of the splits was led by Reinhart Ruzo. He was accused of stealing money from the church, denied the accusation, and he and his followers formed their own group.

The *Oruano* still meets in Katutura now, but in recent years it has been politicized. Most *Oruano* members, like most members of the Red Band, appear to be members of the DTA political party. Others who are not DTA members have evidently been forced out of both the *Oruano* and the Red Band.

5. See the discussion about stereotypes later in this chapter, where the results of LeBeau's (1991) analysis of ethnic occupational stereotypes are discussed. Her research found that ethnic and gender occupational stereotypes still feature prominently.

6. An opportunity sample of 127 Owambo street corner worker men found that the median number of years they had been on the street looking for work was two years, the median number of years in Katutura was also two years, and the median age was twenty-six years.

7. Compared to the informal-sector activities of other African cities, Katutura and Windhoek have a small informal sector. Many licensing laws make informal sector activities illegal or prohibitively expensive if licensing requirements are met. These laws and others were enforced during the apartheid era and worked to severely limit informal-sector development. Since independence, some laws have been changed and others now go unenforced. In March 1989, a Hawkers' Association was founded to represent the interests of street vendors, and one of the association's goals is to lobby for changes in municipal laws which affect hawking.

8. !*kharib* is a fast-fermenting home-brew drink made from yeast, peas, and sugar which often has a much higher alcohol content than beer. *Tombo* is a beer brewed from millet (*mahango*) which is more nutritious, contains less alcohol, and is especially popular with the Owambo.

9. Taken from *Last Steps to Uhuru* by David Lush (1993:24–25).

10. Drinking to get drunk may be compared with drinking as a social activity. However, it is my observation that many Katutura people drink to become drunk and that it is less of a social activity than an activity to produce intoxication.

11. It should be noted that not all cases reported for the central region are Windhoek residents.

12. See Cogill and Kiugu (1990) for a detailed description of the health indicators discussed in the text. Percentages reported for Katutura were run from the HHNS dataset by the author. Katjiuanjo et al (1993) has very complete data on demographic and health data for Namibia, but it is unfortunately not yet available for only Katutura.

13. The data for the case study was collected in 1990 by Debie LeBeau who subsequently undertook a research project on street children in 1992 and 1993.

14. Preston et al (1993) is the major study on Namibian war-affected people to be conducted to date.

15. In 1990, the HHNS found returnees in 27 percent of Katutura households, and in 1992 the RADIO Survey found 4 percent of households with returnees nationwide. Results reported in the text for the returnee and stayer population in Katutura are based on my analysis of the data from the WAP project.

16. Spouses of household heads include partners who are married and those living together.

17. The association, which has its origins in the German colonial period, died out during World War I. It was reestablished in the 1920s and has been in existence ever since. The association had a large meeting hall in the old Main Location. A Commando Hall was built in Katutura, and this has a designated marching area demarcated by piles of rocks. The color red is symbolic of the Herero blood spilled in the German-Herero War of 1904–05. The *Otjiserandu* is organized into troops (local groups) in the towns and reserves. There is only one troop in Katutura, and it is one of the largest in the country. Men wear military-type uniforms, while women wear specially designed Herero dresses as their uniforms. Women and young people have only been admitted to the organization since the mid-1950s.

Otjiserandu leaders have military ranks such as field marshal and general. On Maharero Day (now called Herero Day), in August every year, troops of the *Otjiserandu* from towns and reserves throughout the country gather in Okahandja (a town north of Windhoek), where they visit the graves of Herero chiefs. It is an unofficial national day for the Herero. There can be little doubt that this association serves the important social function of reinforcing Herero solidarity and establishing and maintaining social relationships among the Herero people. In recent years, it has evidently been politicized, and most members are alleged to also be supporters of the DTA. Poewe (1985:333) comments that it should not be surprising that the Herero formed a politico-religious movement. She sees it as a reaction to "their suffering, social dislocation, and cultural upheaval."

18. Other teams were Black Africa (Herero and Tswana), Blue Heaven (Damara), and Morocco Swallows (Damara).

19. No detailed investigation of migrant workers was made. On the basis of observations and some interviews, however, the situation appears to be similar to that Harries-Jones (1969:303–4) describes for the Copperbelt. The Urban Area-oriented characteristics of home boy groups are confirmed by Banghart's data (1969:130–37).

20. According to Greenberg's classification of African languages, Bantu is the major linguistic subfamily of the Niger-Congo language family.

21. Not everyone appreciates hearing English spoken. One of the NISER researchers ordered a soft drink in a bar in English. A rather large Afrikaner gave him a hard time for speaking English. He said, in Afrikaans, to the rather small Damara researcher: "What are *you* doing speaking English, boy?" and the researcher responded by saying: "I'm speaking English because it's the official language of our country, and I'm a Namibian, not a boy!" Then he ran for his life.

22. Gordon (1990:75) comments on the same phenomenon by reporting the case of a Namibian German woman with liberal political views. "The rumour then circulated amongst her acquaintances that the reason for her 'left-wing tendencies' was because she had 'coloured blood' and this gave her a guilty conscience." It is more likely that the local belief was that "blood is thicker than water"; they did not think she had a guilty conscience, but that she was supporting one of her own.

Main street leading into Katutura from Windhoek. Note the Compound in the left background and the housing office on the right (1968).

Housing in Katutura (early 1970s)

Rental house in old Katutura

Rudolf Schimming's service station in Katutura (1969)

A complex housing the community hall, cinema, and library in Katutura (1969)

Barman serving customers in the municipal beerhall in Katutura (late 1960s)

Cooking in the backyard (1968)

Damara couple on their wedding day (1968)

5

The Katutura
Household

PEOPLE LIVE OUT their lives in arrangements that attempt to meet their various social, psychological, economic, physical, and nurturing needs. The household may be viewed as a social, production, socializing, and economic unit.[1] This chapter covers various features of household life in Katutura, including information about dwellings, social structure, economics, problems and resources. The generally accepted definition of a household is a group of people who eat and sleep together. They share some if not all of their meals, and they sleep in rooms that are on the same dwelling site. The household concept places the emphasis on the demographic aspect of people sharing a dwelling site; the members of a household are people living together at the time of the data collection. Sometimes, information is also given on household members who are temporarily absent.

Household Dwelling Information

Dwelling site and household site are complementary concepts. In Katutura, a dwelling site (a lot or *erf*) is usually demarcated by a fence and/or other physical boundaries such as a wall. The dwelling site has amenities such as a dwelling structure(s), water, sewage, electricity, and a yard, as well as other resources. People as members of households control, pay for, and are responsible for maintaining these resources and thereby give a social as well as a physical definition to the site. The dwelling site is also part of the urban geography of Katutura and has an impact on the social concept of the household.

When Katutura was built, it was a new type of location for Windhoek. In all previous locations, people built their own houses. In Katutura, the municipality built about 3,000 houses prior to and during 1959, and an additional 1,000 were built in 1967. The houses were rented to applicants who qualified under the municipal apartheid rental policies described earlier.[2] The ability to qualify determined whether or not you could rent a house. These individual houses, with two, three, or four rooms, had unfinished walls, no ceilings, and no inside doors. They had water and sewage. Electricity could be connected if the necessary fees were paid; about fifty houses had electricity in 1968.

Prior to 1966, a few African businesspeople purchased houses from the municipality at a cost of about R640. The municipality stopped selling houses in 1966, and no *erven* could be purchased. Six private owners had previously built modern houses with the municipality's consent. No further individuals were allowed to build private houses in 1968, and some informants thought that the owners of the houses already built would be forced to sell them to the municipality; they were, however, permitted to keep them.

Approximately 4,000 houses were available for occupation in 1968. In addition, dormitory-type quarters (the single quarters) were available for up to about 1,000 men who did not qualify or want houses or did not want to lodge in someone else's house. There was also a compound, consisting of barracks, which accommodated up to 3,600 Owambo men working on the contract labor system.

The physical dwelling and the place where it is located influence many features of household and family life. The most striking thing about the physical appearance of Katutura before was that most houses looked identical, although they were painted in different colors. On the front door, each house had a letter and number that indicated the ethnic section in which the house was located (for example,

D1/21—Damara Area One, House Number 21). The houses were all located on plots of more or less the same size, with fences around them. About 80 percent of the houses had four rooms arranged in a similar pattern. The sitting room usually had a table and four chairs. Visitors were entertained in the sitting room or in the backyard. Visitors normally announced their arrival at the backdoor. Most people slept in beds, and some bedrooms had dressers and clothes closets. If people cooked inside, there was a wood-burning stove (which was expensive) or a small primus stove in the kitchen; few people had electricity. In all other cases, meals were prepared outside over an open fire in the backyard. Few people made improvements to their houses such as installing ceilings or plastering walls, not only because of the financial burden involved, but also because the municipality did not reimburse them for these improvements, and since they did not own the houses, they could be evicted at any time. The municipality owned the houses and rented them out on a monthly basis. Personal photographs and calendars were frequently used to decorate walls. Damara and Nama women sometimes put up sewn rectangular pieces of cloth called *Stricklappen* or *blomlappe* with sayings in Nama and German, mostly of a religious nature.

Types of Dwellings in Katutura Now

Katutura now exhibits considerable diversity in the type of dwellings available, quality of housing, and size of houses. Katutura no longer has a uniform appearance: dwellings are large and small, new and old, owned or rented, in excellent condition and badly in need of repair, modern houses, traditional Owambo stick houses, and there are also squatter settlements with various types of informal dwelling structures, including tents. Combinations of the above may also be found on the same dwelling site. Some dwelling sites are large, others are small. A minimum of 11,610 dwelling sites were identified in 1991; some of these sites have more than one dwelling structure on them.[3]

The contract labor hostel barracks was demolished in 1987, when it was deemed impossible to rehabilitate, and no large hostel dwelling for workers now exists in Katutura. The contract labor system itself was abolished in 1975.[4] The men who lived in the compound found accommodation in various parts of Katutura such as the single quarters and Shandumbala, and many went to live in Hakahana, which was specially built for men who had to leave the compound. Today, many of these men share rooms and live in households without conjugal partners or wives present.

The Single Quarters is still part of the Katutura housing scene, despite the efforts of some to have it condemned. Some households occupy large modern houses, while others live in the rear of an old rented municipal house or in an abandoned vehicle chassis or a makeshift room. Some households rent rooms in houses, while others rent space out back, where they put up temporary informal housing.

Estate agents now advertise houses for sale in Katutura, NGOs have low-cost housing developments, private building contractors develop housing sites, and the National Housing Enterprise (NHE) builds new housing as fast as possible. National policy is to provide dwellings for Katutura households rather than site and service schemes where people erect/build their own house. How long this policy will be viable only time will tell.

About 82 percent of the total housing in Katutura is rental housing. Of the rental housing, about 44 percent are municipally-owned houses, about 21 percent are privately-owned, and room rentals account for another 17 percent. About 16 percent of Katutura housing is privately owned and occupied (see Table 14). Median monthly housing costs in 1991 were R120 for municipal housing, R140 for private housing rental, R60 for room rentals, and R200 for private housing cost (numbers calculated only for respondents reporting a cost; about 12 percent of households reported no housing cost) (see Table 15). The median number of rooms per house is four, and the median amount of time on the dwelling site was about five years in 1991 (Table 16).

The HDL survey (1988) asked heads of households to describe the quality of their housing environment. Seven features were identified (neat, clean, comfortable, quiet, light, size, and safety), and respondents ranked each attribute on a scale as (1) positive, (2) in between, or (3) negative. For most attributes, about half the households rank the attributes as positive, about a quarter of households are in between, and less than a quarter are negative. Size, safety, and noise are the most negatively evaluated housing attributes (see Table 17). After independence in 1990, the municipality embarked on a major road-tarring and streetlighting program for Katutura, which should have raised the level of housing environment satisfaction.

Household Social Structure

The following discussion defines and describes the types of households found in Katutura. These definitions are relative and not hard and fast realities of social life, but they are useful because they reflect some of the various ways Katutura people have chosen to organize their lives. Other topics included in this section are the size and composition of households, data on the heads of households, and a comparison of Katutura households before and now.[5]

The categories of people in a household may include conjugal (male/female couple relationship) couples who live together or may be married (church marriage, magistrate's marriage, or traditional marriage), relatives, nonrelatives, adults, and children. The information on household members is taken from the point of view of the household head, and how the people in the household are related to the head. Information on households headed by males and females is presented in this chapter. Households headed by males include those conjugal households formed around a nuclear or extended family as well as households without the conjugal relationship. Female-headed households are not based on a conjugal relationship. This distinction between conjugal and nonconjugal families distinguishes fundamental differences in household types that were important in Katutura before and still are now. Many comparisons are made between these two types of households.

Some dwelling sites have more than one household living on them. For Katutura before, only 2 percent of dwelling sites were occupied by more than one household, and they were all female-centered households. In Katutura now, 19 percent of dwelling sites have more than one household sharing the dwelling site. The average number of households per dwelling site in Katutura now is 1.6, which means an average number of eight persons per dwelling site (about five adults and three children). For comparison, one household occupied a dwelling site in Katutura before, and the average number of people was about four. Katutura households and dwelling sites now have about twice as many people as before. Almost 85 percent of the multiple household dwelling sites consist of two households. There are three patterns of almost equal representation on the two-household dwelling sites:

1. Two female-centered households or a female-centered with a conjugal household.
2. Two male-centered households or a male-centered with a conjugal household.
3. Two conjugal households.

For households on dwelling sites with other households, the household heads are asked if they are related to the other households. About 65 percent say they are related to people in the other households.

Types of Households

Four types of households are found in Katutura:

1. Nuclear household including a man and woman with/without children.
2. Extended household consisting of a man and woman with/without children, and relatives or friends of the man and/or woman.
3. Male-centered including a man with/without children, with/without relatives or friends.
4. Female-centered consisting of a woman with/without children, with/without relatives or friends.

Nuclear and extended households are based on a conjugal couple (man and woman cohabiting) who may be married (traditional marriage, church marriage and/or civil marriage) or living together. Male and female-centered households may be the result of divorce, death of a spouse, choice not to marry or live together, and other circumstances not of one's choice. These households are centered around a man or woman who is the household head and who lives without a partner residing on the dwelling site. Conjugal households include both nuclear and extended households.

The above discussion sounds rather formal and static. In reality, the composition of a household changes, reflecting the life cycle and the personal tragedies/successes in people's lives. Children grow up and leave their family, people quarrel and move away, loved ones die, and people move due to lost jobs or improved employment opportunities. The changing nature of the household/family structure and the relative stability/permanence of the household/family structure is discussed in the following sections.

Basically, two kinds of households are found in the Katutura of yesterday and today: those based on a conjugal union between a man and a woman (nuclear or extended household), and those centered around only one person (male or female-centered). Almost equal numbers of these two household types were found in Katutura before: 54 percent were centered around one person, and 46 percent were based on conjugal unions. Katutura now exhibits a significant change in household types: 40 percent centered around one person, and 60 percent based on conjugal unions.

Three types of conjugal unions were found in Katutura before and now: living together, legal marriage (church and magistrate's marriages), and traditional marriage. In all three instances, the establishment of a conjugal union is usually preceded by one or more children being born to a couple. After the birth of a child, the couple may decide to live together and the relationship may continue on that basis permanently. Later, either by individual choice when enough money has been saved for a church marriage, or due to outside pressure, a legal or traditional marriage may be arranged.

Living Together

The percentage of households based on living together in Katutura before and now has remained about the same at 20 percent. The characteristics of a living-together union before and now also have not changed. These characteristics are:

1. It is not necessary to obtain permission from relatives in order to commit oneself to a living-together union.
2. The establishment of such a union is a private matter, and essentially it concerns only the man and woman involved. There is no ceremony and no bride is given.

3. Permission for a church or traditional marriage may have been refused by relatives, but this does not prevent the couple from living together.
4. In a living-together union, the woman usually maintains rights over any children born out of the union. If the couples separates, the woman usually keeps the children.

A man and a woman in a living-together union are more or less free to conduct their private and public life as they deem fit. A partner does not have the right to question his or her copartner's behavior. This freedom, which both men and women have in a living-together relationship, is one of the reasons that many men gave for not wanting to marry in church. Either partner in a living-together relationship is free to terminate the relationship at any time. Informants say that the longer a living-together relationship lasts, the less likely it is to be terminated.

In most instances, the residence pattern for this type of union is that the man initially moves into the woman's house. As long as the house is registered in the woman's name, she has the right to ask the man to leave at any time. In Katutura before, 11 percent of the living-together households were headed by women. This residence pattern was a reflection of the fact that women were allocated houses much more easily than men, and that a woman and her children were, in many instances, the permanent part of the family. Although the official policy was to discourage permanent black urban settlement, women were able to obtain houses in Katutura more easily than men. Women were excluded from many of the regulations with which men were forced to comply, and it appeared that it was easier for women to qualify for urban residence than it was for men. A common pattern before was that a woman would have a child, be allocated her own house, and the child's father or another man would then move in. Later, the house was transferred into the man's name.

Among all ethnic groups, the man took the initiative if there was to be a change from a living-together relationship to one of the other types of conjugal unions. African women informants consistently said that they do not initiate a discussion about getting legally or traditionally married. Women have means other than putting the question directly if they wish to influence their partner, such as pressure through relatives and friends. The situation has not changed significantly in Katutura now, except that women have a much more difficult time finding a house or room to rent.

In Katutura before and now, there is very little stigma attached to or social sanction against couples living together. No one would refuse friendship on this basis. On the other hand, being married does carry some social status. Ministers exert pressure on members of their congregations to marry in church. In the Lutheran Church, couples living together must sit at the back of the church, and they are not allowed to take communion. In the Lutheran and Roman Catholic Churches, living-together couples' children are not accepted for baptism. Some Damara informants said they had yielded to this type of pressure and married in church "for the children's sake," that is, so that the children could be baptized and receive a baptismal card. The African Methodist Episcopal (AME) Church adopted a somewhat different attitude. They encouraged church marriage and did not permit living-together couples to take communion, but a couple could have their first three children baptized. After the third child, no further children were accepted for baptism until the couple married in the church. African ministers complain that it is difficult to exert pressure on African couples in Katutura because it is so big; they say it is easier to exert pressure on couples to marry in church in smaller towns.

Unless otherwise noted, the following information applies to Katutura before and now. Nama speakers call a living-together relationship *soregu* or ‖*âgu*, and ‖*â!gammeb* (a love marriage). Most informants say the woman has the right to all children, and the biological father is responsible for supporting the children. In Katutura before, Damara men and women entered into living-together relationships more frequently than members of other ethnic groups. Also in Katutura before, legal marriage was the most common type of conjugal union for other ethnic groups, but for the Damara, living together made up more than 50 percent of their unions.

In Otjiherero, a living-together union is called *otjiwoteka*. The father of a woman living together in *otjiwoteka* has guardianship over any children who may be born out of the union, and the biological father essentially has no say in the raising of the children. These children belong to the *oruzo* (patrilineal descent group) of their biological father, although this has little functional significance today. If the biological father wishes to claim custody of a child from an *otjiwoteka* union, he must give the child's mother *katjivereko*. *Katjivereko* is payment consisting of a cow and a calf, or the equivalent in money. If the payment is accepted, the biological father may take the child, and he will usually send it to a female relative to raise. The mother's father has the option, however, of agreeing or refusing to let his daughter accept the *katjivereko*. He may refuse and say that he wishes the biological father to marry his daughter.

There is a strong sentiment among the Owambo that living together is "not the right thing to do." This attitude could perhaps account for the fact that Owambo women had the lowest percentage of living-together unions in Katutura before.

Legal Marriage

About 24 percent of conjugal households in Katutura before were based on legal marriage (church marriage and magistrate's marriage). In Katutura now, about 47 percent of conjugal couples report being legally married. The major reason for the substantial increase in legal marriage is of an economic nature. People in Katutura now have more money and more sources for money. The cost of marriage is not as great a barrier as it was in the past, and this is reflected in the greater number of legal marriages.

Case Study 8 below describes one couple's magistrate's marriage and their eventual break-up.

CASE STUDY 8: Magistrate's Marriage—"Short marriage"[6]

As a young girl in Owambo, I worked in the fields and went to school. The main thing we did in school was basket making; the boys made mats (*oshiinda*). Most of the time we played at school. At home I pounded *mahango* and the boys looked after cattle. I went to boarding school at Ontananga until 1959 and finished my ninth year of schooling. I started my tenth year of schooling at Oshigambo, but decided to go and work as a teacher. I taught for a while at a place where my brother lived, but there was a water shortage, so I went back to my parents' kraal. In the middle of 1960, I decided to visit my sister in Katutura. At that time the life was very bad because whenever you wanted to go somewhere you had to have a permit. I applied for a permit to go to visit in Windhoek and got it.

I did not want to return to the north. I stayed in Windhoek for two months, and then the police caught me. I spent a month in jail and then the police made me return to Owambo. My sister applied for another permit for me, and when it came I went back to Windhoek. My permit expired and I had to spend the whole day in town in order to hide from the police. Life was difficult.

In 1966 a man wanted to marry me. I agreed to get married, but we decided to make a short marriage at the magistrate's. Although getting married in church is very important to the Owambo people, we decided to get married at the magistrate's. I wanted the paper so I could get permission to stay in Windhoek. Then, when the police stopped me, I just showed them the paper with my husband's name on it. But our life was not very good. He beat me so much it affected my health. I had two daughters. Each time I was ready to give birth, I went to my mother's home in Owambo to give birth. My mother told me to return to my husband even though he was beating me; that women have to suffer from their husbands. We stayed married for thirteen years and then I decided to leave him. I found out he had a wife in Owambo, and I was tired of the beatings. In 1979, I went back to Owambo and stayed for a year; then I went to stay with my mother's brother on a farm near Otavi. Then I returned to Windhoek to discover my husband had told the magistrate I had died and he had married another woman.

I returned to the house where I had stayed before in Katutura. The house belongs to my elder sister, but she does not stay there. I stay in the house with my three children (a son and two daughters). Another female relative also stays in the house with her two children. We are four adults (two of my children are grown-up) and three children. The life in Katutura is very hard. I am not finding a job. I have never been able to find a job. I completed nine years of schooling and I taught school for a short while. I am the only one in this household who earns any money. I sell *oupana* (meat). With the profit from selling the *oupana*, I pay the house rent and buy food. I am the only one who is looking after all these people. My biggest problems are money, crime, employment, food, and housing. I still want to get a job, but I am over fifty years and I do not think I will overcome these problems. I think the government should help us.

In Katutura before, having a marriage certificate had its advantages. It was easier for a couple to obtain housing in Katutura. Furthermore, some white employers gave dependents' allowances and paid the house rent, but only if their employee was legally married and could produce baptismal cards for his children. Therefore, marriage and baptismal certificates were economically advantageous for some. Another aspect that African women pointed out was that since they did not carry documents or identification papers as the African men did, a marriage certificate was a useful document. Police officers made routine checks in Katutura, and a woman without any documents was treated with suspicion. The police might suspect that she was another of the women from the reserves who had come into Katutura illegally. If she had a marriage certificate she was in a better position to argue her case.

The degree to which Western ideas and values about marriage influenced people in Katutura before was difficult to determine. The Windhoek area was racially, socially, culturally, and economically stratified. Berreman (1964:245) observed that in situations where there is a dominant group, the members of the subordinate group "characteristically come to value positively many of the norms of the dominant group." Legal marriage, especially church marriage, was the ideal among the white population and was sanctioned by the church, which was strong in the country. Whites also directly encouraged their black employees to get legally married because it was the right thing to do, or indirectly through the influence of the ideal pattern of the higher-ranked white category. Today, the influence of Western cultural patterns is even stronger due to the wide availability of television (about 50 percent of Katutura households have televisions), and videos and television programs that are primarily American and European in their cultural orientation.

Church Marriage

For Katutura people of yesterday and today, church marriage is the most important type of legal marriage. It is the only type of conjugal union that involves a public ceremony and establishes new kinship obligations and responsibilities. A church wedding must be planned in advance, since the banns of marriage must be read in the church three weeks prior to the ceremony. The cooperation and participation of a number of people are required. In most cases, the permission and sanction of relatives must be obtained.

A church marriage requires a bride price. With the exception of traditional unions, of which there are relatively few, church marriage is the only conjugal union that requires a bride price. In the urban situation, where descent groups are absent, the bride price is an acknowledgment of the bride's status. The higher her status (prestige), the higher the bride price to be paid. In part, it is compensation paid by the groom's family to the bride's family for having raised and trained their daughter. The more training and education she has received, the greater their loss when she marries, and the higher the bride price that must be paid. If the woman's training is interrupted by a man, he must then also compensate the family. A Damara mother said her future son-in-law would have to pay a high bride price because he prevented her daughter from finishing her studies by getting her pregnant.

In Katutura before, an average bride price amounted to about R100 (n = 32), but it could be twice as much or even more for an educated and trained woman. Today, the bride price may be as high as several thousand rand. A church marriage cannot normally take place without the bride price having been paid, and without a church marriage, the mother retains all rights over her children. They are hers, and they are her old-age insurance in the sense that they will help provide for her when they begin working. When the couple marries in church, the father acquires rights over any children subsequently born. Thus, while filiation to a descent group is not a function of urban church marriage, filiation to the father's or mother's family is.

Church marriage is an expensive proposition for a man and his family. Besides being required to pay the bride price, the groom is supposed to purchase the new clothes for the ceremony for himself and the bride, pay the majority of the expenses for the marriage celebration, provide housing and food for friends and relatives from out of town, and take care of various other expenses. In Katutura before, a minimum estimate for all these expenses came to about R250, and could prove to be even more expensive. Today, the cost may be ten times as high, or higher. As most men do not have this amount of money, couples first live together, planning to marry in church once they have saved enough money. However, a larger percentage of couples can afford the costly church marriage today than was the case in the past.

Clan and lineage considerations do not play a role in partner choice, since descent groups have little significance today. Köhler (1959:66), writing about the Herero in the 1950s, reports that the patrilineage was no more than a family name at the time. The Damara apparently never had clans or lineages, while the lineage and clan groupings of both the Nama and Owambo are of minor importance. However, people who share certain names or are too closely related will not be permitted to marry. The Owambo tradition of a man being responsible for his sister and her children was strong before, and it still is today. A colleague described how his married sister, resident in Katutura, had run up an R800 bill that he was required to pay.

African informants of all ethnic groups said that the ideal residence pattern after a church marriage would be for the bride to move into the groom's house. Since, however, few unmarried men have houses, this pattern is usually not possible. If the couple is already living together (in the woman's house), there is no change of residence. Men often have houses registered in their name after marriage, since they are nearly always acknowledged as household head. In Katutura before, the man would be listed as the new head of the house and the couple listed as legally married when the marriage certificate was shown at the Katutura housing office.

A church marriage is a time of celebration. Many people, women in particular, come to church services especially to see weddings. More traditional brides wear long Victorian-style dresses made from white material. Others wear modern wedding dresses. The groom always wears a dark suit and a tie. If in any way possible, couples will attempt to arrange for a car to bring them to church and take them away. Many congratulations and gifts are given and many photographs are taken. A celebration with more than enough to eat and drink usually follows the ceremony.

Over the years, the number of church marriages has increased. Table 18 shows the number of church marriages for periods between 1933 and 1968. The increase in church marriages, beginning in 1959, probably reflects a desire for security because of uncertainty over residence in the old Main Location, since a marriage certificate would facilitate getting a house in Katutura. The increase in church marriages in Katutura between before and now probably reflects the greater ability for some to pay for church marriages today.

Herero Marriage Customs

Herero church marriages were less frequent in Katutura before than they had been in the past. Of the 165 church unions contracted by Herero men and women, only 18 percent took place after 1961. The significance of this drop is especially dramatic when compared to the figures for other ethnic groups; the percentage of unions established after 1961 lies above 58 percent for every other ethnic group. The main reason for the drop in the number of Herero church marriages is the establishment of the *Oruano* Herero separatist church in 1955. *Oruano* ministers were not licensed marriage officers, and they could therefore not perform a legal church marriage. The *Oruano* church remained close to Herero traditions, and it is likely that it recognized the Herero traditional marriage. Members of the church do not disclose details about the *Oruano*.

Herero call any type of conjugal union, with the exception of living together, *orukupo*. A legal marriage is called *wakupa koveta*, *koveta* being a Hereroization of the Afrikaans loan-word *wet* (law). The Herero language does not linguistically distinguish between a church marriage and a magistrate's marriage. In the case of a church marriage, the bride price (*otjitunya*) is paid in money; many Herero consider church marriages to be a town phenomenon, and money is therefore deemed to be more appropriate; money is also paid in rural areas, though. Negotiations to obtain the permission of relatives of both the groom and the bride are necessary for a church marriage. The procedure is, however, much less complicated than it would be in the case of a traditional Herero marriage. All that may be necessary is to obtain the permission of the woman's parents once the consent of the man's parents has been obtained. A few examples of cross-cousin marriage were encountered among older Herero informants. Arranged marriages are no longer made today.

The traditional Herero marriage also requires the *otjitunya* (bride price). This is usually paid in cattle (one ox and five cows), although money can be substituted. The *otjitunya* is paid during the three-day marriage feast (*omukandi*) that is usually held in a Herero communal area. Herero informants stated that there have been traditional marriage celebrations in Katutura. On one occasion in 1967, I saw Herero women dancing the *outjina* in the old Main Location. Since this dance is only performed at traditional marriage celebrations, it is likely that a traditional marriage was being celebrated.

Even Herero who have lived in town for a long time are not immune to pressure to contract traditional marriages. One middle-aged Herero man who was born in Windhoek found himself promising his best friend, who was dying at his home in a reserve, that he would marry his daughter. The daughter was only 21 years old, and the Herero man was living with another woman. He asked a Herero chief, a relative, to try and convince his dead friend's family that such a marriage would be a mistake, and the chief succeeded.

The same couple may contract one or more types of conjugal unions over time, and some couples have two different types of conjugal unions. A couple might start their relationship by living together, but then contract a magistrate's marriage due to social pressure. Later, when they have saved enough money for a church marriage, they may even marry in church. Herero who still wish to contract a traditional marriage may also find it necessary to get legally married on account of the need for a marriage certificate.

Damara/Nama Marriage Customs

A church marriage is highly valued by Damara and Nama people. A Damara informant explained that "a traditional marriage was something special and mystical in pre-European times," and said that today, in the absence of traditional marriage, the church marriage is viewed in this way. Virtually all Damara and most Nama church marriages take place in the Lutheran Church. They are conducted by a minister who speaks Damara/Nama. The ceremony usually takes place on a Sunday, after the normal church service. The couple comes to the front of the church, where the minister asks them a few questions, blesses them, and marries them. After the ceremony, the couple, accompanied by relatives and friends, goes to the house in which they will live or to the house of the bride's mother. In Katutura before, couples collected money on a "marriage walk" as was the custom among the Owambo, but that custom is no longer practised in Katutura.

When the couple arrives at the house, they may have to wait at the backdoor until money has been collected for the marriage celebration. A female relative of the bride, her mother's sister or her own sister, may stand in the doorway and refuse to let anyone enter the house before the money has been collected. The wedding party takes place later that afternoon and evening. Usually, the bride remains in the bedroom during the marriage feast, where she spends the time talking with friends and trying to look shy and solemn.

Nama speakers call any type of conjugal union, with the exception of living together, !gammeb (marriage). A church marriage is called !khō!oms (to clasp hands). It is customary to pay a bride price (!gu‖gab[7]), although this is not actually a Damara tradition. Informants said the term may refer to food eaten at the marriage feast. Another term for bride price is bruidie (possibly from the Afrikaans word for bride—bruid). The parents of the groom may also be asked to bring a cow (apagomas). This cow, for which money cannot be substituted, is intended to symbolically replace the animal that was slaughtered when the bride was born to make the carrying-skin in which the mother carried her child on her back. However, practical considerations usually make it impossible to adhere to this custom in Katutura today, and the groom's parents purchase meat from the butcher.

A man can approach a woman's parents directly and ask to marry their daughter. He may also send a female relative to the girl's mother to announce his intentions. If the parents indicate their willingness to discuss the matter, the man usually sends one or more of his female relatives to conduct the discussions on his behalf. It may be necessary for these relatives to make three or four trips to the girl's mother's house before they will finally be allowed in to begin the discussions. It is naturally more convenient if the man has female relatives in town, but relatives may make a special trip to town in order to conduct the necessary discussions.

If a Damara or Nama woman marries in church, she becomes part of her husband's family. She is not supposed to return to her mother if she has domestic problems, and is expected to approach her husband's mother for help if necessary. If the husband has a complaint regarding his wife, he is supposed to go to his wife's mother to complain. A married man has the right to beat his wife, and she is not supposed to run away if he does. Some Damara women said they did not want to marry in church because their husbands would then beat them and there would be nothing they could do about it.

Owambo Marriage Customs

For the Owambo, the ideal conjugal union is a church marriage. A man who was not married in church is referred to as "not having a house." Owambo church weddings are most frequently held at the Lutheran and Roman Catholic Churches. The ceremony is similar to that described for the Damara and Nama, except that it is conducted in Oshiwambo.

The Owambo marriage walk no longer takes place in Katutura, but is still practised in Owambo. The couple, together with friends and relatives, assemble in a small group and walk to the house where the couple will take up residence. For each step the couple takes in the direction of the house, one of the leaders of the group, usually a female relative of the bride—ideally her sister—must collect a small sum of money. This money is saved and given to the couple later. As they proceed to the new couple's residence, people join in from time to time, tossing a few coins and singing and dancing. Sometimes, a flag announcing the marriage is carried. Once they arrive at the residence, the groom's father must contribute some more money, the amount being determined by the bride's female relative who was in charge of the walk, after which the bride may sit down on the bed. All the money is given to the couple to spend as they like.

Owambo men pay a bride price (*iigonda*) to the bride's parents. The usual procedure is for the bridegroom to give this money to a female relative who then presents it to the bride's parents. The bride's parents keep part of this money for their private use, and part of it is contributed toward the cost of the wedding party. There must be meat at the *ohango*; this is provided by the groom and his father. The *ongombe yohango* (the wedding ox—*Oshindonga*) ought to be slaughtered just before the wedding feast to provide the meat required, but this custom is seldom adhered to in town owing to the practical difficulties. The marriage feast is either held early on

Sunday morning, before the wedding ceremony, or on Sunday afternoon, after the ceremony. Permission for the marriage is obtained through discussions between the parents and relatives of the bride and groom. Only the parents and relatives are supposed to be present at these consultations, which usually take place at the house of the bride's parents.

Owambo informants said that if an Owambo man married a woman from a different ethnic group, the children are nevertheless considered to be Owambo. There are, however, certain difficulties, since the Owambo have a matrilineal descent system, and the children have no link into the matrix of Owambo genealogical and kinship relations if the mother is non-Owambo. Urbanization and other factors have had an influence on the Katutura family. Gibson (1991:19, 50, 51), reporting on her Katutura research on Oshiwambo women, describes the shift in authority from the wife's eldest maternal brother or brother to the husband in conjugal households where the couple is married. She argues that the parental reproductive family has taken over some of the responsibilities of the extended matrilineal family. She attributes the changes to urbanization, capitalism, administrative factors, and Christianity.

Magistrate's Marriage

Couples living in Katutura before and now contract magistrate's marriages. A magistrate's marriage (civil marriage) is a legal union, and the couple receives a marriage certificate. This certificate satisfied the Katutura housing authorities in the past, and also represented a document that was useful in other dealings with the authorities. A magistrate's marriage is inexpensive, does not require the posting of banns, and requires little preparation. Unless one or both persons are under age, the marriage can be performed without the consent or permission of anyone, and the couple can make all the arrangements themselves. There are no obligations as regards a bride price, a marriage celebration, the purchase of clothes, and the asking of permission from relatives.

A magistrate's marriage is a private ceremony and a private decision that involves only the couple themselves. I observed three magistrate's marriages in 1968 and all three couples came alone, without friends or relatives. Clerks, who serve as witnesses, said that most people come alone. The main reason for such marriages is the need for a document to obtain housing in Katutura, some other administrative purpose, or to qualify for some benefit paid only to those who are legally married.

Among all African ethnic groups, a magistrate's marriage is spoken of as a cheap marriage and is considered less binding than a church marriage. Most people who enter into this type of relationship have been living together and probably decided to contract a magistrate's marriage due to pressure. The tremendous increase in magistrate's marriages between 1957 and 1964 (+322.5 percent) was a direct response to the situation created by the threatened closure of the old Main Location (see Table 18). Many people thought they could improve their chances of being allocated a house in Katutura if they had a marriage certificate; in fact, many were told to get a certificate.

Traditional Marriage

Traditional marriages, based on customs predating the colonial era in South West Africa, are relatively rare today. Such unions were not recognized as legal unions during the colonial period. Only fifty-two traditional unions were found in Katutura before (3 percent of the conjugal households and 2 percent of all households). The Damara and Nama no longer contract traditional marriages. Owambo informants said they knew of no Owambo resident in Katutura who would even consider contracting an Owambo traditional marriage, although it was said that traditional marriages are sometimes contracted in rural Owambo. A study of marriage among the Ndonga Owambo (Tuupainen 1968) indicated that traditional marriage was rare, living together was frequent, and that some couples were married in church. The importance of the church among Owambo people is usually given as the reason why traditional marriages no longer exist among the Owambo.

The only ethnic group in this study that still contracts traditional marriages are the Herero, although this custom is practiced by only a few. Arranging a Herero traditional marriage is a long and tedious process; informants said it may take eight years or even longer to complete. Many male and female relatives of both the man and woman who wish to marry must approve the union. Should any of these relatives refuse to consent, the procedure is halted. The father of the man who wishes to marry must then go personally and ask those relatives to reconsider and approve the marriage. It may be necessary to resolve old quarrels and settle unpaid debts before relatives give their consent.

Conjugal Partner Choice Patterns

The choice of a conjugal partner is an important decision, and one aspect of that choice is whether the partner comes from the same ethnic group (ethnic endogamy) or a different ethnic group (ethnic exogamy). If the total number of endogamous conjugal unions is expressed as a percentage of the total number of conjugal unions, then an ethnic endogamy percentage of 85 percent can be calculated for Katutura before (82 percent for couples living together and 86 percent for legally married couples). These percentages are high and show—not surprisingly—that ethnic groups had rather strong boundaries, limiting the choice of conjugal partners in the past. In Katutura now, the endogamy percentage for all types of conjugal unions has dropped to 58 percent (61 percent for legally married couples and 52 percent for couples living together).[8]

Households Headed by One Person

Although there are some important exceptions, the household based on a conjugal union is a widespread ideal throughout the world. Situations where people are unable to establish and maintain a conjugal relationship and raise children are often associated with serious social problems. Katutura before and now represents one example of such a situation.

In Katutura before, 55 percent of the households were headed by one person. The female-centered household made up 36 percent of households, and 19 percent of households were male-centered. Divorced, separated, or widowed persons were heads of about 4 percent of households, most of which were female-centered. The only dwelling sites with more than one household recorded were sixty-one female-centered households where the daughter of the female household head also had children of her own. In Katutura now, households headed by one person make up 40 percent of households. Female-centered households make up 25 percent of households, and male-centered households represent 12 percent of households.[9] Divorced, separated, or widowed households make up 10 percent of total households, most of which are female-centered.

Female-centered households have the lowest household incomes of all household types, and the greatest difficulty with limited resources. Gibson (1991:52) describes how Owambo women who are heads of households make use of their matrilineal links (to brothers, maternal uncles, and aunts, etc.) for assistance with material support, inheritance, and accommodation.

In Case Study 9 below, a woman who is the head of a female-centered household describes how difficult she finds her situation.

CASE STUDY 9: Female-centered Household[10]

Life is not going very well for me. I am suffering because I don't have money to buy food. My daughter makes ice cream to sell, but she can't make any profit. She is still a young woman and she doesn't have a job, and she is just sitting around at home without having anything to do. She was working as a domestic worker before independence, but now all she can do is this job at home of selling ice cream. The problem about jobs is worse now than before. To get jobs now you have to have higher qualifications and experience. The problem now is that the living standard is too high so we cannot afford to look after our children.

I am doing a house-cleaning job, but I don't make much money. I can't manage to support my children and pay their school fees and other expenses. I have eight children and they are still in school. I am looking after the whole household, but the money I earn is not enough. I would prefer to have a husband in the house. The problem is the man who gave me these children did not want to marry me; he just gave me children, then left me. I wanted to marry in order for my husband to help me to look after the children because it is hard for me to support my children alone.

Life is hard. For example, one of my sons has twelve years of education and another has eight but they can't find work. The one with twelve years of education was looking for a bursary but could not get one. Now he is at home not doing anything.

Size of Households and Categories of Household Members

Households in Katutura have become larger. Each household type shows a small increase from before to now. Looking at all household types collectively, the average household size before was about 4.4 people, while the size today averages about 5.0 people. The increase in people by household type from before to now shows both change and continuity in family structure. The number of children per household has significantly increased only in the case of female-centered households, the number of relatives per household has not significantly changed and is greatest for male-centered households, and nonrelatives have become a much larger household category for conjugal and especially male-centered households.

The number of children by household type has remained about the same for conjugal households from before (2.6 children per household or 52 percent of household members) to now (2.7 children per household or 50 percent of household members). Male-centered households have the fewest children with about one per household accounting for 38 percent of household members before and 27 percent now. The number of children in female-centered households has increased the most from a before figure of 2.6 to a now figure of 3.4; children make up 69 percent of household members now.

Relatives were a significant part of male-centered households before (20 percent) and they still are, accounting for 23 percent of household members. Relatives account for a small percentage of household members in female-centered households, accounting for 9 percent before and 6 percent now.

In Katutura before, nonrelatives were an important household member category for male-centered households, accounting for 10 percent of household members. Now their importance has doubled to 20 percent of household members. Nonrelatives in conjugal households have increased from 1 percent before to 9 percent now.

Household Economics

Money and jobs have always been a problem for people in Katutura households. In Katutura before, due to apartheid policies, there were limited employment opportunities. People approached the Windhoek job market at a great disadvantage. Most were employed in the formal sector in Windhoek as unskilled workers with a typical monthly salary of R70 for men (85 percent of employed men earned R70 per month or less). They worked as messengers, making deliveries, doing cleaning and general janitorial work, and they made the tea and coffee for their white employers. Some men earned an above-average salary working as bus and truck drivers, mechanics' assistants, and construction workers. A few men worked as clerks and salespeople in places catering to African customers. There were about forty African school teachers working in the Katutura schools, and about forty African businesspeople (all men). Opportunities for women were even more limited. Employment as domestic servants and selling beer in *shebeens* were the major opportunities for women to earn money. On account of these apartheid realities of life in Katutura before, it was not surprising that most households did not have enough money to get by from month to month. At the same time, there was very little formal unemployment. As stated earlier, unemployed men without a permit to seek work or reside in Katutura had to find work or risk being arrested by the police and "endorsed" out of Katutura.

A cost-of-living survey was conducted in June 1967 (Venter 1967). It was calculated that the minimum a Katutura household of five (father, mother, and three children) needed to live on was about R100 per month.[11] This minimum household budget is shown in Table 19.

If R67 is taken as an average monthly salary for a man in 1968, and allowing that his wife also worked part-time as a domestic servant and earned R15 per month, the household income was R82 per month, which was R22 below the calculated minimum. Female-centered households had less income, and therefore found it extremely difficult even to come close to this budget. This validated the frequent complaint of people that they did not earn enough money and explained why many women brewed beer to earn a little extra. Lack of money was a frequently discussed topic, and people with money were admired and often discussed. In conjugal households, irrespective of the type of union, the woman virtually always handled the money. The view about household economics in Katutura before was that men were employed in the formal sector primarily as unskilled workers, women earned money in the informal sector, and most households had about the same amount of money available.

Sources and Amounts of Household Income in Katutura Now[12]

Monthly household income is today derived from a variety of sources. Formal-sector employment is the source of income for 59 percent of households (see Table 20). Informal-sector employment is the only income source for 16 percent of households, and a combination of informal- and formal-sector employment accounts for 7 percent of household income. Some 14 percent of households depend solely on income from pensions, welfare/support payments, and savings. About 3 percent of households depend on other people for their income.

Both the formal and informal sectors of the economy have changed considerably over the last twenty years. Formal-sector employment now includes a much greater diversity of occupations than previously available for blacks under apartheid, but the informal sector has changed even more significantly. In Katutura before, the informal sector was almost insignificant, while at least a quarter of all households depend on the informal sector to some extent for their household income today.[13]

Two case studies describing the problems experienced in getting by on scarce resources are presented below. Case Study 10 describes the situation of a household based on a conjugal relationship, while Case Study 11 shows the situation of a female-centered household.

CASE STUDY 10: How a Couple Gets by on Scarce Resources[14]

We are a very poor family. We have five children and three are going to school. There is also a relative of mine staying with us. He got only two months ago a job. Before that time, my husband was the only breadwinner. Two years we built a house with the loan my husband got which we still owned. After the completion of the house my husband paid the payments of the loan till now.

Seventy-five percent of his salary went to the payments of the loan. We managed to build only the half of the house with that loan. I applied to the government for loan at the Ministry of Local Government and Housing, and we are busy upgrading the house. Together with both loans it is difficult to survive until the end of month.

We are new in this area and we don't know anybody where we can borrow some money or food. Normally my husband borrows some money from his friends at work and I pay it back from the money I got by selling ice cream and making clothes. This always does not work and then I ask for assistance from my family. Our monthly food for the month lasts only three weeks. Paying the payments of the loans and paying the payments of the accounts and buying if it got finished is the toughest of all because the payments increments if not paid and the food is a necessity for everybody.

Sometimes I try to ration the food into portions and at least it last till the fourth week. Our finance is so limited because my husband's salary got finished with all the bills and accounts. There are times that I don't even buy food for the month. In that case we survive by buying food like kilo of sugar, kilo of maize, one loaf of bread and a kilo of meat on the daily basis. For next day you have to struggle to be able to eat. If you are lucky, you got something, and if not, you stay without it.

CASE STUDY 11: How a Female-centered Household Gets by on Scarce Resources[15]

I am in my late forties and was married about fifteen years ago. I have seven daughters and one son, from whom two daughters are married. None of my daughters are educated or they leave the school in their secondary level. Only two are still attending the school. I am with my mother, who is also pensioner.

The normal total income for this household is about 400 to 500 rand per month. I am a domestic worker and receive about 300 rand per month because I work for three different people. My mother's pension is also added to this; it brings the total income to that amount. All my daughters have children; the second eldest has four children; third one also four kids; fourth one has three kids; third last one has two and the second last one has one kid. The eldest is staying with her husband at her house.

About eight years ago I was working for a German couple. Before they left for Germany, they gave some amount of money with which I bought this house with about R1,000. The life is really difficult for us and we are struggling. My husband and me are divorced for a long time now and all this time I am the only one who looks after the family. There are times that we went to bed without eating anything. Sometimes the kids went to school without any food.

But still we are surviving. There are times that our monthly supply increases, especially when my daughter plaits hair for extra income. But most of the time our food in stock got finished within two weeks. If we are lucky enough it last for three weeks. At times like this I normally borrow money from my employers and paid them back at the end of the month. Sometimes I borrowed food or money from my friends, neighbors and relatives. Every end of the month I buy at least twelve kilos of maize, sugar, and flour and I weigh it into portions that at least a kilo of each is available everyday. This way the stuff last for three to four weeks. But most of the time accounts and bills does not allow, and each time we have to fall back to borrow money or food.

As a means of earning extra income, the women in Katutura organize groups which they call Savings Clubs. Women come together and form a club where they contribute a minimum amount of money. They open a joint account and deposit every month this amount. The number of members is unlimited because the more the members are, the higher will be their capital. A member is allowed to borrowed some amount of money, depending on the availability of it, and she should pay it back with little interest at the end of the month together with her normal monthly contributions. At the end of the month they withdraw all the money and divide it among them.

Another way of getting extra income is a group of people, say two to three, come together and contribute a minimum amount of money. One person takes that money, and at the end of the month they contribute again. This time another person takes the money, and it goes on until all the people has received his/her share.

The median monthly income from all sources for all households in the KAT1991 is R800 (mode = R700), but there is considerable variation in monthly income, as evidenced by the high standard deviation that is almost equal to the mean (Table 21). When examined by household type, female-centered households have the lowest median income (R500) and extended households have the highest (R966). However, all household types also have considerable variation in monthly income, which is a reflection of their very different economic circumstances.

In Katutura today, every household must deal with the problem of unemployment (including both the formal and the informal sector). With the exception of male-centered households, all households have about one person who is seeking work (see Table 21). Male-centered households have fewer people not working because they would not be allowed to remain in the household without work, and they are younger and more eager for jobs.

Sources and Amounts of Household Expenses in Katutura Now

The minimum household subsistence level (HSL) for September 1991, based on Potgieter (1991:68), is R767. It should be recalled that the HSL is not considered adequate for a household of five people to meet its monthly expenses, and that the University of Port Elizabeth researchers recommend the minimum to be 150 percent of this figure. Thus, the previous discussion for households above and below the median income level of R800 would seem to separate households that are above and below a minimum survival income.

The usefulness of the HSL has been debated. Some feel that it is a bench mark against which employers may calculate a minimum wage for the black workers. The HSL is used here in order to gauge a relative poverty datum line. Some households in Katutura are clearly doing better than others, and about half the households in Katutura are living well below a minimum survival level. Women are still the money managers in conjugal households, and for those households living below the HSL, money management is a challenging exercise.

Major expense categories for Katutura households are shown in

Table 22. The expense categories, in order of priority, are food (27 percent), rent (21 percent), clothing (14 percent), transportation (11 percent), utilities (10 percent), medical (6 percent), and other expenses (11 percent). The "other" category includes such costs as savings, entertainment, remittances to other households, and alcohol. The percentages of monthly expenditures are remarkably constant for all types of households, including households with an income lower than and higher than R800 per month. A few patterns emerge from a study of Tables 23 and 24. Female-centered households spend the greatest percentage of expenditures on rent; nuclear and extended households below R800 spend the greatest percentage on food; male-centered households below R800 spend the greatest percentage on clothes and alcohol; extended households above R800 spend the greatest percentage on utilities; and male-centered households above R800 spend the largest percentage on transportation.

Food Consumption and Purchasing

With food accounting for almost a third of household expenditures, a profile of household food consumption is revealing. No detailed food consumption data has been collected, but basic food consumption/purchase data is available from the 1991 Katutura survey and the HDL (1988). The presentation of this information provides a general overview of household food consumption patterns. Based on information from the HDL (1988), major food categories consumed are as follows: *basic foods* (maize-meal/corn, rice, potatoes, brown bread, and white bread) are consumed on a daily and weekly basis by most Katutura households; *dairy products* (including milk, thick milk, powdered milk, butter, and margarine) are consumed by about three quarters of households on a daily and weekly basis; *meat products* (including tripe, beef, mutton, chicken, and fish) are consumed on a daily and weekly basis by somewhat over half the households, with the exception of fish, which is eaten less often; and *vegetables/produce* (including fresh and canned vegetables, fresh salads, fresh and canned fruit) are consumed by less than half of households on a daily and weekly basis (see Table 25). The most common foods eaten on a daily basis are maize-meal, brown bread, and dairy products. Other very popular food items are sugar, cooking oil, instant coffee, tea, and beer.

The data from the HDL (1988) indicates that both home-brewed and bottled beer are the most popular alcoholic beverage consumed by people in Katutura households. Home-brewed beer is consumed daily by people in 13 percent of households, bottled beer in 8 percent, and wine in 5 percent. Home-brewed beer is more popular with people in households that are below the median income (see Tables 26 and 27).

Comparisons

When the above four food categories are compared, contrasts and comparisons may be made for household food consumption. In old Katutura, a greater percentage of maize-meal and brown bread, slightly less dairy products, more tripe and less beef/mutton, and less fruit/produce is consumed than is the case in new Katutura. The food consumption patterns of conjugal and female-centered households do not differ significantly, but male-centered households consume less of most basic food categories on a daily basis than other household types. Households above the median household income level consume significantly greater percentages of most food categories on a daily basis.

Household Resources

The move to Katutura was not without some improvement in household resources. The old Main Location had pit latrines and a few communal water taps. In Katutura, all houses had water taps and water-carried sewage in an outhouse at the rear of the dwelling site. In Katutura before, few houses had electricity, and most households used wood or paraffin for cooking fuel. Seeing people having a meal around cooking fires in the rear of their houses in the evening was a very common sight in Katutura before. It was also very common to see a haze of smoke from wood-burning fires lingering over Katutura in the evenings and mornings. Preparing food in a kitchen was not very common before, although some households did have paraffin stoves and bottled gas inside. The situation in Katutura now is quite different. As Katutura developed into new Katutura, many houses were built with water and toilets inside the house.

Only about 13 percent of Katutura households now use firewood all the time, and few households use charcoal, paraffin or bottled gas (see Table 28). About three quarters of households have electricity, and ownership of electrical appliances is common. Over 80 percent of households have refrigerators, electric irons and radios; about half the households have electric stoves, electric kettles, and televisions; and smaller percentages of households have stereos and hotplates (Table 29). Access to electricity has resulted in quite a change in household activities (such as watching television and videos), food preparation, and convenience. About 28 percent of households have a motor vehicle. Thus, the quality of life for many has significantly improved since the apartheid years.

Household Problems

How difficult is life for people in Katutura households? One way of attempting to answer this question would be to examine the relative ranking of various problem areas. In 1968, the overwhelming major problem confronting Katutura households was lack of money. As part of the KAT1991 survey, people were asked about the most serious problems that confronted their household. Household heads ranked nine problem areas on a scale from 1 (not very serious) to 5 (very serious). Table 30 shows the results of their answers. The four most serious problems, as indicated by the median scores, are debt/money, housing, food, and job/employment. An examination by household type does not reveal any difference in answers about the importance of these four problem areas. Education problems are moderately important for all households (median = 3). However, problems with children are more serious for female-centered households, while crime is a more serious problem for male-centered households. Health, crime, and domestic issues are the least important problem areas. Certain household problem areas (children, food, debt, and employment) were more serious for households in old Katutura than they are in new Katutura. For households with an income of less than R800 per month, all household problem areas are more serious, with the exception of crime and domestic problems, which are the same.

Household heads were asked if they thought they could overcome the most serious of these problems; 68 percent responded yes or maybe, and 32 percent said no (see Table 31). When asked whose responsibility it was to solve the most serious household problems, 40 percent of household heads answered that it was the responsibility of the government, 38 percent said it was their own responsibility, and 14 percent indicated they thought it to be the responsibility of local government and the national government. Table 32 shows two interesting attributes of those households that have more problems; they think they will overcome them and it is their own responsibility to solve their problems.

Notes

1. Unless otherwise indicated, information for Katutura now (1990–93) is from the Katutura 1991 survey, and information for Katutura before (1968–70) is from Pendleton (1974). Various other datasets will be referred to, such as ENERGY (1991) and HDL (1988); dates refer to when the data was collected. See chapter 2 for a complete description of the datasets.

2. There were two rental schemes in operation in Katutura in those days. Unmarried women who were heads of households paid about R4 per month for a four-room house. Men who were employed and heads of households had their rent paid by their employers. The employers were required to pay about R8 per month for house rent for their African employees directly to the municipality, and were entitled to recover about R5 from the African employee's salary, depending on his salary scale. This was a new scheme instituted by the municipality in an attempt to recover some of the claimed financial loss suffered in connection with the construction and maintenance of Katutura.

3. The Windhoek municipality's town planning department advised that there were 11,874 defined dwelling sites on *erven* in Katutura and 300 tents in July 1993 (personal communication).

4. For a recent study of the contract labor system see Hishongwa (1992); one of the first studies on the system was Voipio (1972). The negative aspects of the system have been commented on in many books and articles. Some of the major complaints were low wages, lack of workers' rights, the inability to bring one's family, abuse and exploitation of workers by white employers, lack of job security, lack of recourse in the event of job-related injuries, and, within the Owambo society, many social problems related to the absence of so many adult

men from households. Voipio, writing about the late 1960s, reported that as many as 50 percent of the adult male population could be absent from Owambo on labor contracts at any one time. Many men, young and old, went on labor contracts because of the perceived need for money and employment. Chiefs participated and even encouraged participation in the system in the past because they received payments from labor recruiters for supplying contract labor workers. In the past, many farm workers were Owambo contract workers; today, few farm workers are Owambo men. Many Owambo men continue to migrate seeking work, but they do so today with freedom of movement and more workers' rights.

5. I have decided to talk mainly about household rather than family. The household is a concept that refers to the people who are actually residing together. It may include a family, but in many cases members of a family may reside elsewhere in other households. For example, children of a family may be sent to live with relatives who reside in other households, and people in a household may actually be members of various other families. It should be clear from the text whether reference is being made to a household family or to people in a family who do not reside in the same household.

6. Case Study 8 is from an Owambo woman in her fifties living in the Owambo area of Old Katutura.

7. The literal meaning is to slaughter the !gus (the loincloth) at the wedding in order to achieve intimacy with the bride.

8. From the 1968 period, patterns in conjugal partner choice can be seen when all four types of conjugal unions are combined (the relevant data comes from Pendleton 1974:154–55). Owambo and Herero women had an insignificant number of unions with men from other ethnic groups. Their ethnic endogamy percentage was 95 percent. Damara women had a significant number of unions with men from every ethnic category. They contributed an average of 47 percent of the exogamous partners for every other group. Seventy percent of the exogamous unions with Damara women were couples living together, while the overall average is 47 percent. Of the unions with Owambo men, 84 percent were living together, which conformed with the Owambo ideal of only contracting legal marriages with Owambo women. Nama women had 50 percent of their exogamous unions with Damara men, and coloured women had 43 percent of their exogamous unions with men from that group.

Men in the Owambo and other ethnic group categories had the lowest ethnic endogamy percentages for men, and both contracted a large percentage of their exogamous unions with Damara women. There are more women in all ethnic categories, with the exception of the Owambo and other ethnic group category. Men in these two categories were forced to look elsewhere for conjugal partners, and since there were 12 percent more Damara women than men over the age of fourteen at that time, this result is not surprising.

9. Pendleton (1990:43) reports that female-centered households made up 18 percent of Katutura households in 1988. This percentage underestimates female-centered households, because some are included under multi-family

households as defined in the HDL project. Cogill and Kiugu (1990:14) report 36.2 percent female-headed households. They may have overestimated female-centered households by classifying some households as female-centered although there is actually a partner present. Based on re-running of the dataset for the HHNS, 60.4 percent of the sample was drawn from old Katutura, which may have biased the sample, since many more female-centered households are found in old Katutura (26 percent in new Katutura and 39 percent in old Katutura). They report that 7 percent of female-centered households have partners who visit occasionally. The figure for KAT1991 of 25 percent female-centered households should be valid.

10. Nama woman in her sixties living in the Nama area of old Katutura.

11. As part of the racial economic ideology of apartheid, the cost of living for a black family was less than that for a coloured or white family. It was thought that blacks needed less because they had a different lifestyle, and therefore needed less money to get by.

12. It is generally acknowledged that it is difficult to collect accurate income and expense data. The income and expense data for KAT1991 was collected carefully, but should be interpreted with some caution. In order to assess the overall accuracy of the income and expense data collected, I calculated a variable called surplus by subtracting total expenses from total income. Some 25 percent of households have a negative surplus, indicating that income is possibly underestimated, expenses overestimated, or the household operated at a deficit during the month this data was collected, requiring the use of savings or borrowed money. There is, however, no clear pattern regarding which households have a negative surplus.

13. The section on work status in chapter 4 contains a description of both the formal and informal sectors of the economy.

14. Case study from a Damara couple living in Soweto in 1993.

15. Case study from a Damara woman in her late forties living in the Damara area of old Katutura.

Independence Avenue leading into Katutura (1993)

Squatter shacks in Katutura (1993)

Former municipal house in old Katutura. Note the old house number on the door (1993)

Private residence in Luxury Hill, Katutura (1993)

Minibuses ready to depart for Owambo (1993)

Municipal bus (1993)

Selling firewood on the informal market in Katutura (1993)

Food stall in the Single Quarters (1993)

6

Katutura
Urbanization

THE GROWTH OF the locations in Windhoek is a story of the movement to town of people who previously lived in the communal areas,
on commercial farms, and in other towns in Namibia.[1] This movement and relocation of people to town, the process of urbanization,
has been going on for almost a century. The attraction of Windhoek
has always been especially strong.[2] As the administrative, political,
and social capital of Namibia, it has always had more to offer
migrants than any other town in the country. The reasons people
state for coming have been consistent over the years. People come for
jobs and to make money, and Windhoek has more of both than any
place elsewhere in Namibia. Frayne (1992:16–17) reports that although
the population of Windhoek represents only about 10 percent of the
country's total population, the town has about 42 percent of the country's formal-sector employment available. Jobs and money, however,
are only part of the story.

Life in town has certain qualities that make it different from rural
life. Town life is modern with music and lights, it offers the possibil-

ity for education, meeting people, taking advantage of opportunities, and the excitement of men/women and bars/night life. In many ways, town life is subsidized. In the rural areas, people often have to carry water, grow their own crops, take care of livestock, build their own houses, have very limited opportunities to make money, and deal constantly with issues of rural social life such as kinship relationships. In Katutura, water and sanitation are more readily available, food is nearly always bought or shared with those who buy it, many have electricity, access to inexpensive health services, educational opportunities, radio and television entertainment, *shebeens* and *cuca* shops, and most people have housing. Even those who cannot find a job and money usually do not leave. They stay, hoping to find work, they hustle, buying, selling, trading, and, some, stealing. But they stay, and more will keep coming for the above reasons.

In the past, the growth of the population in the old Main Location and Katutura was artificially controlled by regulations and the police, first under the German colonial administration, and later under South African apartheid control. It was only during the decade prior to independence that the restrictions on urban migration were abolished. The rapid growth of Katutura in recent years indicates the extent of repressed urbanization. Between 1970 and 1987, the Katutura population doubled from 25,464 to about 55,000; it almost doubled again in only five years between 1987 and 1991. The growth of the Katutura population from 1987 onward is unprecedented in the history of Windhoek. The growth of the Katutura population in absolute numbers and percentages, from the earliest figures available to the present, is discussed in this chapter. Factors affecting population growth and migration are discussed, and reasons for migration are evaluated.

Katutura Before

In Katutura before, people lived in considerable uncertainty about their ability to remain in town. There was always the fear of being "endorsed out" of the urban area owing to loss of job or documents. People could not buy or sell land, own their own homes, or leave town on trips without jeopardizing their right to residence in the

Windhoek area. But the black population of Windhoek continued to grow despite the apartheid regulations. The steady growth of the black population in absolute numbers and percentages is shown in Tables 33 and 34.

People also considered Katutura to be their permanent home, despite the insecurity in which they lived. One hundred informants in the informant sample were asked: "Do you plan to stay in Katutura for the rest of your life?" and 74 percent said they did. Informants emphasized that there were better employment opportunities in Windhoek, more to see and do, and they liked the life in the area. Informants who did not plan to stay permanently explained that they were only in town to work and make money (15 percent), and intended moving to a smaller town or the reserves later because the cost of living was lower there. One informant explained that she owned property on a farm, but although she had lived in the town for thirty-seven years, she owned no property in town. Eleven percent of the informants were undecided about their future residence. A further indication of urban commitment concerned the upbringing of children. Although informants mentioned many bad influences of town life, such as heavy drinking, violence, rough life, and lack of respect, most wanted their children to grow up in the Urban Area. Their reasons were that children learn the modern way of life in town, have better education opportunities, town life makes them more aware, and there are better employment opportunities.

In the past, those who migrated to Windhoek first stayed with either parents or close kin, for example, mother's brother, father's sister, a sibling, cousin, or affines. While the old Main Location still existed, they simply built their own houses. In Katutura it was more difficult; the only housing available was municipal rental housing, and one had to qualify to be able to rent a house. Some people came to Katutura to go to school and then remained, others came to get married, some were transferred, but most came looking for work.

During the apartheid years, an attitude commonly held by non-blacks was that blacks wanted to go to the communal areas when they retired or stopped working. This, of course, was also official government and municipal policy. Black people did not have this attitude. The only people who expressed a strong desire to retire to the communal areas were Herero. They owned cattle, sheep, or goats in the reserves, sent money regularly to pay their grazing fees, and said they would be happy living in the reserves. But opinion was divided even among the Herero. Of forty-one Herero who were asked: "Would you be happy living in the reserves?" half said they would not. Many Herero owned cattle in the reserves, but had no intention of residing there permanently. One informant owned cattle and paid grazing fees, but had not visited the reserves for more than ten years. The sale of cattle provided income for some, and the ownership of cattle plays an important role in Herero social relationships. Informants frequently spoke of inheriting cattle, especially from their mother's brothers. Most Owambo contract workers also returned to the northern communal areas when they no longer worked, but this was due mainly to the fact that it was unlikely that they would be able to obtain a permit to reside in Katutura permanently.

Table 35 shows the place of origin or last domicile of employed African men from the various ethnic groups in Katutura before. On the basis of the totals of Table 35, the general picture that emerges is that 41 percent of the African men were born in the Windhoek area, while a further 33 percent came from other towns in Namibia. The remaining 25 percent came from the communal areas and the white-owned commercial farms. An important exception to the pattern were the Herero, with 35 percent originating from Herero communal areas. No information on black women's place of origin was available for Katutura before. It was estimated that more than half were born in the Windhoek area.

Katutura Now

Detailed information on urban migration was collected in 1991. The following section reports responses given by adults (persons over sixteen years of age) who migrated to Katutura; they make up 81 percent of the Katutura population, with the remaining 19 percent being born in Katutura or the Windhoek area. The major reasons people gave for leaving other areas were lack of jobs (37 percent), no money (32 percent), inadequate schools (7 percent), and poor social life (5 percent) (see Table 36).[3] A larger percentage of men than women left on account of jobs and money. Reasons other than jobs and money that are more important to women include pregnancy, school, social life, and other unspecified reasons, which accounted for 24 percent of responses (Table 37). An analysis of the reasons by place of prior residence reveals certain patterns. The major reasons for leaving commercial farms were inadequate schooling (39 percent) and poor social life (10 percent), and major reasons for leaving other towns and communal areas were jobs and money (58 percent and 78 percent, respectively) (Table 38).

Jobs and money are also the major reasons people give for coming to Windhoek (71 percent), with education the second highest response category (10 percent) (see Table 39). Jobs and money represent the major response category for men migrating to Katutura (82 percent); it is also the largest response category for women (69 percent), but women have more additional reasons than men for coming to Katutura, such as education, housing, and visiting.

The last residence of migrants prior to moving to Katutura was frequently a communal area (67 percent), often Owambo (50 percent). A smaller percentage of migrants come from other towns (16 percent), and the smallest percentage migrate from farms (3 percent). About 14 percent of the migrant population come from other areas. Some moved to Katutura from the old Main Location. Others are from Angola and elsewhere. Probably about 7 percent are returnees. Those who come to Katutura do so for the same reasons (jobs, money, education), but the relative importance of the reasons differs by place of last domicile. Those from the communal areas come primarily for jobs and money (79 percent). Education is more important for people from other towns (15 percent) and especially important for people from the commercial farms (39 percent), which reflects the lack of adequate educational opportunities on the commercial farms. People identified various other reasons such as medical facilities, housing, and modern life, but the percentages are uniformly small.

Migrants were asked three questions to measure the extent of urban/rural contact of migrants (see Table 40). Respondents were asked if they still had fields and/or livestock in the rural areas; 69 percent of the migrants said they did not. Of those respondents who said they did, 6 percent have fields, 10 percent have livestock, and 15 percent indicated that they have both fields and livestock. The second question pertains to the number of times the rural area is visited per year; the average number of visits per year is about one. The third question asked whether money was sent to family living outside Windhoek; 13 percent said yes, 29 percent said sometimes, and 58 percent said no. Of those who send money outside Windhoek, only 3 percent send money to family on farms, while 7 percent send money to family in other towns, 63 percent send money to family in Owambo, and nearly all of the remaining money sent outside Windhoek is sent to other communal areas. The average amount of money sent outside Windhoek, by family, is R156 per month.

People were asked who they stayed with when they came to Katutura. Their responses clearly show the importance of family and friends. Only 10 percent indicated that they were on their own, while 59 percent stayed with family, and 20 percent stayed with friends (see Table 41). People were asked to indicate what they would do if life went badly for them in Katutura. About half the respondents (46 percent) said they would return to their previous residence, 20 percent said they would move to another area, and 34 percent said they would stay in Windhoek (see Table 42).

Case Study 12 reports the urban migration experiences of an Owambo man and his efforts to find employment.

CASE STUDY 12: Problems of Urbanization as Seen through the Eyes of a Migrant[4]

I stayed in the Katutura compound in 1976 and later in 1979 I stayed in the Single Quarters. I have four children from my girlfriend and two children from another woman.

The first time I came to Windhoek, I was given a permit for seven days to visit Windhoek to see whether I can get employment. When I didn't find employment I had to return to Ondangwa to get another permit to return and look for employment again. If I found employment I was supposed to go back to Ondangwa to fill out forms that showed that I had employment in Windhoek. This process continued until the contract system was abolished.

My children were always sent to Owambo to live with my grandparents because I had no place where they could stay. They used to come and visit me here in Windhoek. When they came to visit me in

Windhoek, then they had to stay with relatives who had houses in Katutura.

The first time I stayed in the compound I didn't have a card because I wasn't employed. I had to use my friend's card and I lived in my friend's room. He used to go out first and then pass the card back through a hole in the wall. I stayed there with him during the time I was looking for employment. I lived in the compound for about four years looking for employment. I used to work for people who wanted a person to work on weekends or do other private work. Later I stayed in the single quarters, but I never found permanent employment. I used to work for about a month, then the work was finished and I looked for more work. I did this for about twelve years. Sometimes I didn't work for six months. I never got a bonus where I worked even if I worked for six months.

I lived in Windhoek for about seventeen years but never found permanent employment. I didn't marry because I didn't get permanent employment and make enough money. The money I made I used to buy food for myself, transport to work, and I even gave money to relatives in Owambo. The money I got was not enough for me to stay with my family. All the money which I get is only for my unmarried wife and me. But sometimes if I worked for someone for about three months then I could buy clothes for my children who are staying in Owambo.

If I get permanent employment then I shall do my best to marry. The problem I have is that I want to get enough money to build my kraal in Owambo because the government announced that we are no longer allowed to cut down trees with which to build our kraals. If I get enough money then I can go to visit my children, parents, relatives, and friends in Owambo.

The Single Quarters rooms used to be given to one person. Later it was changed so that up to four people stayed in the room. It can be that up to six people are staying in such a room, and even a family may stay in such a room. You could even stay in these rooms with your wife, but if you also want to cook in this room, it is too small. The government changed many things in the Single Quarters. The water pipes were changed and many other things. People can visit freely now.

After independence there came some changes. We can travel freely without requiring permission, and we can walk anytime, anywhere. I like it that nobody is going to ask you for permits any more.

Whites used to chase me away if I came asking for work because they were afraid because we didn't go to school. Sometimes they used to say that their work was not going to be done by blacks or kaffirs because they don't know anything. Sometimes when I walked in the streets then whites would call the police because they said that I would come and kill them or steal their things, which was not true.

I am now hoping for myself that the government will offer employment for people who don't have any work. If they can do it then I shall really be for it. If I get employment from the government then I shall try my best to marry.

Length of Residence in Katutura and Migration

Respondents were asked the number of months they had resided in Katutura. The following discussion applies only to adults and to those who migrated to Katutura (the data was collected in 1991). The mean number of months of residence in Katutura is 28. The migrant population can be divided into the following four approximately equal categories reflecting when they took up residence in Katutura:

1. 28 percent came within the last two years;
2. 23 percent arrived between 2.1 and 5 years ago;
3. 23 percent came between 5.1 and 12 years ago; and
4. 26 percent migrated more than 12 years ago.

This quite dramatically shows one strong indicator of the extent of urban migration to Katutura; about one quarter of the adult Katutura population have migrated within the last two years, and half have migrated within the last five years.

Length of residence is evaluated against the migration questions to identify whether recent migrants differed from migrants who came to Katutura many years ago. Several trends in language/ethnic group patterns are clearly visible (see Table 43). The migration of Owambo people has increased progressively over the years; 34 percent of adult Owambo migrants have come to Katutura in the last two years. During the same time period, the number of Nama migrants has declined steadily. Migrants of the last two years have two interesting educational attributes. They have a higher level of education, with 40 percent having a Standard 10 or higher educational level; however, a large percentage of migrants with no education (23 percent) have also come within the same time period. The largest percentage of unskilled workers have come to Katutura in the last two years (39 percent), and of all workers who have come to Katutura in the last two years, 48 percent are unskilled (see Table 44).[5] The migrants who have come in the last two years have also had difficulty finding employment; 58 percent of these recent migrants are unemployed (see Table 45).[6] The last residence prior to Katutura reveals migration patterns. The number of people coming to Katutura from other towns in Namibia has declined in the last two years (15 percent), while the number of people coming from Owambo has increased over the same time period (36 percent). Jobs and money are consistently major reasons for migration to Katutura; however, the number of respondents indicating they came for school/education for their children increased to 33 percent during the last two years.

Notes

1. I have previously reported some of the results of Katutura urbanization in Pendleton (1991) and Frayne (1992:153–63).

2. Between 1936 and 1970, the percentage of blacks living in urban areas in the southern section of Namibia (those areas in the former police zone) increased from 14 percent to 41 percent, with Windhoek accounting for about 25 percent of the total for most of those years (Pendleton 1974:19). These percentages were calculated on the southern section population only, and did not include the total black population from the northern areas of Namibia.

3. Frayne (1992:17) makes an important observation when he reports that an unskilled urban migrant who only finds work occasionally may in fact be quite a successful migrant when the alternative is considered. "Income from working a millet field of 2 hectares in the rural north for 80–100 days a year yields an equivalent of approximately R3.12 to R4.00 per adult working day." Occasional unskilled work will earn a man that much, and probably more.

4. Owambo man in his early thirties living in a makeshift room in the Single Quarters in 1993.

5. The 48 percent is calculated by taking the number of unskilled workers (129) and dividing it by the number of workers (267) that have come within the last two years, resulting in a percentage of 48 percent.

6. The 58 percent is calculated by taking the number of unemployed persons (146) and dividing it by 251 (the number of migrants within the last two years).

7

Stratification

I PREVIOUSLY DESCRIBED the Windhoek area as having attributes of both class and caste stratification. Each racial group resembled a caste with boundaries limiting employment (blacks were restricted to unskilled occupations), marriage (marriage and sexual relationships between blacks and whites were illegal), and residence (blacks had to live in Katutura). Mobility between castes was virtually nonexistent.[1] Any mobility that did exist was limited to caste groups that exhibited features of socioeconomic stratification that allowed individual mobility. Social distance between racial caste groups was artificially maintained by social customs and separate facilities. The ideology of separateness was the apartheid policy of the South African government as implemented in Windhoek and Katutura, and racial and ethnic group identity was emphasized in all areas of life. The government used "racial" and ethnic identities to exploit and limit the potential of people. One of my strongest realizations about the functioning of apartheid was that it created a strong feeling in people that they were different, that people in one group differed culturally and socially from people in other groups. Racial and ethnic group consciousness was strong, because so many of the social and cultural boundaries in the society coincided.

The social and cultural boundaries are no longer as strong, and they do not coincide to the same degree as previously. Apartheid as an ideology has disappeared. However, the structure of apartheid still stands, and the racist attitudes of many people may still be experienced. The social structure of Windhoek can no longer be described as a caste system without mobility between groups. Employment, marriage, residence, and facilities are no longer determined by apartheid regulations, but the structure of apartheid has left a strong imprint on the society. The existence of Katutura in itself is a strong statement about the legacy of apartheid. One of the big changes that can be observed in Katutura today is that it is socioeconomically stratified to a much greater extent than was the case in Katutura before.

The differentiation of people and households on the basis of wealth, quality of housing, socioeconomic status, type of household, area of residence, and other factors is one of the major developments in Katutura now. This differentiation stands in sharp contrast with the situation before, in the old Main Location and Katutura, where the situation of all people and households was more or less similar. It is ironic that the end of apartheid opened previously closed doors of employment, opportunity, and freedom, while at the same time it made life more difficult for some than it was in the past. For many, there are new opportunities, but for others, their inability to compete for better paying formal-sector jobs means that they must compete in the informal sector or go hungry.

On the other hand, there is a growing new elite "comprising much of the existing elite together with an expanded organizational elite, of senior black administrators, politicians and business people" (Tapscott 1993:13). The lifestyle of this new elite has little in common with that of the majority of Katutura residents. Although some members of the new elite live in Katutura in houses appropriate to their position and status in the community, many have purchased homes in some of the best residential areas of Windhoek. In Katutura before, little socioeconomic stratification was apparent. Most people and households had similar resources; most were poor. Katutura had a uniform appearance. There was little occupational differentiation, with the exception of the elite status of a few Katutura residents discussed earlier.

In an attempt to look at stratification in Katutura now, three themes are discussed below on the basis of data presented earlier. These themes are residential stratification (which compares old and new Katutura), stratification of household types, and economic stratification (a detailed discussion of households below and above the median household income level). Each of these themes demonstrates a different aspect of Katutura stratification today.

Residential Stratification

Stratification in housing areas is clearly apparent when old and new Katutura are compared. To the observer who drives through these areas, old Katutura looks poorer, old, neglected, and rundown. Other features are not so apparent (see Table 46 for details). When type of housing is compared by areas of Katutura development, certain characteristics are found:

1. About equal percentages of housing are owned and rooms rented in old Katutura and new Katutura;
2. About twice as many municipal rentals are found in old Katutura as in new Katutura;
3. Many more people rent privately owned houses in new Katutura than in old Katutura; and
4. Dwelling sites located in new Katutura have more households on them than those located in old Katutura (see Table 47).

The elite area of Katutura, Luxury Hill, is located in new Katutura.

These figures actually tell part of the story of what has happened to Katutura housing over the last twenty years. As additional housing is developed in new Katutura, most of it is privately purchased. Many people are able to qualify for low-cost housing loans because they work for the government; in Katutura before, no government housing loans were available for Katutura and no people (with a few exceptions) were allowed to own houses or land in Katutura. In Katutura now, municipal rental houses still account for more than half the old Katutura housing, while almost half is privately owned. The municipality has tried to remove itself from the housing business by selling off its stock of rental houses; more than half the former rental houses have been sold over recent years. In effect, the burden of providing low-cost housing for Katutura residents is being shifted from the municipality to private investors who rent rooms or houses. For new Katutura residents, the problem is not to qualify for a house under the apartheid housing policies previously applied; the problem is to find a room or house, and to be able to pay for it. The cost for a municipal rental house varied from R8 to R10 per month before; the median cost to rent now is R110 per month.

The ethnic composition of old and new Katutura shows certain differences. The ethnic areas of old Katutura are still primarily ethnically homogeneous, for example, the former Herero area is still almost exclusively Herero, and the same is true for the other ethnic areas of old Katutura. In new Katutura, each area has more ethnic homogeneity than the areas in old Katutura. The percentage of Damara people is highest in old Katutura, and the percentage of Owambo is highest in new Katutura. These percentages reflect the fact that many more Owambo have migrated to Katutura in recent years than people from other ethnic groups. The ethnic composition for the Herero and Nama is about the same. The mean number of months of residence is twice as high in old Katutura (156 months), but this reflects the fact that old Katutura is older. Age, literacy, and occupational skills show no difference between the two areas. People in old Katutura have slightly less educational achievement than people in new Katutura. About 8 percent more people are working in new Katutura, with a higher median income (R630 compared to R503) (see Table 48). There are no apparent differences in fuel use between old Katutura and new Katutura, although perhaps slightly more households in new Katutura use firewood than in old Katutura.

About three quarters of the returnee population live in new Katutura. Old Katutura has about 10 percent more female-headed households than new Katutura, and about 10 percent fewer household members are working in old Katutura. Household heads in old Katutura are slightly less educated and literate than in new Katutura. Household heads in old Katutura are older and earn less money per month; spouses in new Katutura earn twice as much as spouses in old Katutura. People in old Katutura drink most types of alcoholic beverages more often than people in new Katutura (Table 49).

Monthly income for the two stages of Katutura development exhibits a significant difference; households in old Katutura have significantly lower monthly incomes (median = R800) than households living in new Katutura (median = R1,000). Old Katutura is older, more crowded and has households with lower incomes. However, it is quite clear from the data that the amount of money available to a household varies considerably for all types of households within all areas.

Households in old Katutura have a larger percentage of almost all possessions. Although the household income is lower for old Katutura, people have lived in old Katutura much longer than in new Katutura (median of 120 months versus 36 months, respectively), which has enabled households to accumulate possessions. Although household income is lower in old Katutura, they in reality have more possessions.

Household-Type Stratification

A comparison of household types by the two stages of Katutura's development reveals certain findings. Almost equal numbers of conjugal households are found in old and new Katutura. However, 71 percent of female-centered households live in old Katutura, while 67 percent of male-centered households live in new Katutura. When the type of household is compared by above and below the median income, the economically disadvantaged position of female-centered households is quite obvious; 65 percent of female-centered households are below the median household income (see Table 50). There is relatively little difference in possessions when analyzed by household type. About 13 percent of male and female-centered households use firewood. About half the conjugal and male-centered households are above and below the median household income.

The percentage of conjugal households by ethnic group shows no unexpected pattern. The Herero, Nama, and Damara all have more female-centered families than would be expected on the basis of their population proportion. The Owambo have a much smaller percentage of female-centered families than their population proportion would suggest and far greater numbers of male-centered households—the Owambo account for 79 percent of all male-centered households, reflecting a very strong pattern. People in male-centered households are slightly older, have been in Katutura for a shorter period of time, and are slightly less educated than people in other types of households. They also have more unskilled occupations, more unemployment, and lower monthly incomes. Male-centered households consistently have more negative scores on the housing environmental scale. People in male-centered households drink home brew, wine, and hard liquor more often than people in other types of households. People in conjugal households drink bottled beer more often than people in other types of households.

Compared to the stayer population, a much higher percentage of returnees live in male-centered households. The educational level of heads in male-centered households is the lowest of the three types of households, the percentage of heads working is the highest, and the monthly personal income of heads in male- and female-centered households is about R200 per month less than the personal income of heads in conjugal households.

Formal-sector employment accounts for about 60 percent of employment for conjugal and male-centered households; for female-centered households the percentage drops to 44 percent. Female-centered households rely on informal-sector employment and income from "other people and other sources" to a greater extent than do other household types. In conclusion, it is clear that male-centered households are better off than female-centered households.

Economic Stratification: Above and Below the Median Household Income Level

In Katutura before, most households lived at the minimum subsistence level or below it. In Katutura now, there is much more economic differentiation. A larger percentage of households below the median income rent rooms (22 percent) than do households above the median. Almost equal percentages of households above and below the median income own houses; however, most (82 percent) of the houses owned by those below the median income level are old municipal houses located in old Katutura. Households below the median income are more likely to rent a house from private individuals (26 percent) (see Table 51). For all three types of households, renting a municipal house is the most popular method of obtaining housing. However, male-centered households are more likely to rent rooms or a private house than other types of households, female-centered households are more likely to own a house (probably in old Katutura), and conjugal households are more likely to rent a municipal house. When the quality of the housing environment is compared for households above and below the median income, those below the median consistently have more negative scores. About 20 percent of households below the median household income use firewood, and all households above the median have electricity.

People in households above the median household income level have slightly higher levels of education and literacy. Households above the median have much higher percentages of employment; 70 percent of those available to work in households above the median are working, compared to 44 percent in households below the median. The median income for people living in households with above the median incomes is R723; the median for those in households below the median is R319. Households above the median household income have larger percentages of all possession categories except gas stoves, which would be more popular with people who live without electricity.

People in households below the median household income drink most types of alcoholic beverages more often than do people above the median household income (see Table 52). Compared to the stayer population, a higher percentage of returnees (48 percent) live in households with a monthly household income above the median. Income and employment status of household heads and spouses reflects the pattern described above. In households below the median, the percentage of heads who are seeking work is greater, the educational level is lower, and the personal income of both heads and spouses is about three and six times greater, respectively.

When the percentage of household types is compared by above and below the median monthly household income, a significant pattern is revealed. Almost twice as many female-centered households are below the median as are above it. There are, conversely, larger percentages of conjugal and male-centered households above the median. Therefore, a disproportionately larger percentage of poor households are female-centered. On the basis of a comparison of the percentage of all household types, more female-centered and less extended households operate in the negative, but the differences are not great. Households in old Katutura have less of a surplus than those who live in new Katutura, female-centered households have the smallest surplus (median = R74), and male-centered households have the greatest surplus (median = R412). As expected, households below the median income level (that is, below the HSL) are significantly worse off than those above it.

Notes

1. The reader may recall the earlier mention of board meetings to consider applications for reclassification of a person's racial group.

8

Conclusion

IN SOME WAYS, life for people in Katutura has come full circle from the past to the present. In the old Windhoek Main Location, people owned their own houses, there was relative freedom of movement, there were a number of clubs and associations, and even elections. For many who lived in the old Main Location, there was a sense of community. Many restrictions were imposed on the black population, but they were only a hint of what was to come when apartheid was implemented in Katutura with full force. With the closing of the Main Location and the forced relocation of people to Katutura, location life took on new features. With the exception of those who were legally permanent residents, the right to live in Katutura was temporary and dependent on a job and adherence to the myriad of apartheid laws. Private ownership of housing was not allowed, restrictions on residence were imposed, marriage and even sexual relationships were regulated, black employment was limited to largely unskilled jobs, there was little economic stratification, households were raided by the police looking for illegal occupants, and people were subjected to the humiliation and embarrassment of having to be subservient or suffer the consequences on a daily basis. Even the urban geography of Windhoek, with buffer zones around Katutura, had the stamp of apartheid.

Postapartheid Katutura has changed in many ways. People are free to travel, take up residence, and look for employment. About half the housing in Katutura is privately owned, many people build on to their houses themselves, rent out rooms for additional income, and they can sell their house or leave it to their children. Housing and business ownership do not depend on racial classification; they depend on the ability to pay. The ability to pay has, in fact, become a very important factor of life in postapartheid Katutura, and economic stratification has become a reality of life for people in Katutura households. About half the Katutura households are below the HSL, and half are above it. For those below the HSL, getting by on scarce resources is a way of life. Households in old Katutura are not as well off as those in new Katutura, households in Luxury Hill are substantially better off than those in old Katutura, female-centered households have a difficult time getting by on limited resources, and male-centered households in Wanaheda and Hakahana do better than female-centered households. Men in male-centered households have more mobility and substantially fewer dependent children to take care of, which in part explains their somewhat better situation. There are wealthy people in Katutura today, the mayor of Windhoek lives in Katutura, there are many more types of jobs and employment diversity, but there are also many poor and unemployed people.

Looking for work and unemployment are a way of life for many residents of Katutura. About 35 percent of the adult population who want to work cannot find employment, although some of these people have skills and work experience. High unemployment and the growth of the informal sector of the economy are both closely related to the rapid urbanization that Katutura has experienced. The population of Katutura doubled between 1987 and 1991, and it will double again soon. People come to Katutura to live and to find work in the Windhoek area. The largest category of migrants comprises Owambo from northern Namibia, who now make up more than half of the Katutura population. New people arrive in Katutura every day, there are many strangers, and anonymity is much easier today than it was in the past. The rapid urbanization and unemployment have created social problems. Street children are a common sight in Windhoek. Crime in Katutura and Windhoek has never been higher. Many people have become desperate for money, and robberies and muggings occur almost daily; there are gangs that operate out of Katutura, and the *botsotsos* are feared by all. The high consumption of alcoholic beverages such as !*kharib, tombo,* and bottled beer is widespread, and those who have the least resources drink the most. Drinking has been a feature of township life from the first locations, but it has reached unprecedented levels today.

Has the strength of ethnic and racial identity changed from before to now? There is no doubt that the strength of both is less today than it was before, but stereotypes are still strong. However, many boundaries no longer coincide as they did in the past, and this undoubtedly has reduced the significance of ethnic and racial categories. For example, the ethnic and racial endogamy percentage in Katutura today is much lower than it was before, and the areas of new Katutura are much more ethnically integrated than the areas of old Katutura. However, ethnic identity is still the strongest social identity for many who are poor. Those with professional and skilled employment are able to associate with people on the basis of occupational or recreational interests, but those who are poor and unemployed have few social identities other than ethnicity. The death of apartheid has not seen the death of ethnic and racial identities, but it has seen a redefinition of both.

What does the future have in store for Katutura? Is Katutura a location on the way to becoming a suburb? I would like to answer yes, but the reality of the situation is that Katutura will remain a location for a long time yet. The reasons are many. The urban structure of apartheid society is still in place. Half the population of Windhoek lives in Katutura, and few have serious prospects of living elsewhere in Windhoek. The cost of land and housing will keep the poor in Katutura, and the poor are still primarily blacks. Those blacks who achieve upward mobility may choose to remain in Katutura, living in nicer homes on larger lots, perhaps in Katutura's Luxury Hill, or they may move to Luxury Hill in Windhoek or some other Windhoek suburb where they fit in socioeconomically. Many blacks live in Windhoek today, but they are middle- and upper-class people whose employment allows Windhoek residence. Some areas such as Hochland Park (the site of the old Main Location) and Windhoek West are integrated, but most are not. Under the force of economic segregation, racial segregation will continue for the foreseeable future.

Will the urban migration to Katutura slow or stop in the foreseeable future? There is no indication of this happening. On the contrary, there is every reason to believe that it will probably increase. Despite the many rural development projects currently under way in Owambo, the high birth rate and declining infant mortality rates of the Owambo population will ensure that the population will continue to grow at current rates, as will the rest of the black Namibian population. Migration from Owambo is a major reason for the unprecedented growth in the Katutura population, and the migrants will undoubtedly continue to come for a long time. They, together with other migrants from elsewhere in Namibia, will seek jobs and housing in an area unable to accommodate them. The result is not hard to visualize. Visitors to Cape Town are confronted with the vast sea of informal shanty housing accommodating the tens of thousands of people seeking work and housing in that area. The same is true for every metropolitan area of South Africa. The same fate is in store for Katutura, albeit on a smaller scale. There are only a few squatter communities in Katutura today, but there is every reason to believe that there will be more in the future. The ability of the government, the municipality, and the private sector to build enough houses to accommodate the continued influx of people is limited. Frayne (1992:173) estimates that the population of Windhoek may be 450,000 by the year 2010; even if this is an overestimate, the future population of Katutura and Windhoek will grow substantially over the next twenty years. The ability of the formal economy to generate sufficient jobs to provide employment is even more limited than the housing market, and it can be anticipated that the informal sector of the economy will grow substantially in the future.

Smith (1992:316), writing about the postapartheid cities of South Africa, sees little chance for improvement in the socioeconomic circumstances for the blacks living in the townships and shacklands in South Africa. He writes about a future "of class divisions steadily augmenting the racial separation inherited from the past, to produce a city characterized by some commentators as one of 'deracialized apartheid.'"

The above scenario could be changed by large government-subsidized public housing projects, disincentives for urban migration, redistribution of current housing, or utilization of urban land outside Katutura for black housing development. Three low-cost housing developments are currently under consideration by the municipality. The completion of these low-cost housing projects, which will probably be occupied by blacks, will contribute to the integration of Windhoek. Without jobs, however, poor blacks will never be able to afford even low-income housing.

The smaller size of the Namibian population may also mitigate the intensity of future urbanization. However, the Owambo and others have few alternatives to urban migration, rural populations are growing, and the need for jobs and money increases daily. Windhoek is the capital and major urban center of Namibia, it has the strongest pull of all other places in the country. The development of other urban centers with increased employment opportunities might also redirect some of the Katutura migration. One intriguing idea would be to relocate the capital of Namibia to Oshakati, in the heart of Owambo, and develop manufacturing and industry where there is both labor and a large domestic market. Another idea would be to make Oshakati and Windhoek dual administrative centers for the country. When there is again peace, stability, and economic development in Angola, having the capital of Namibia closer to the border might be auspicious. It will be exciting to see what happens in the next phase of Katutura's history.

Appendix

Appendix 1

Details of Surveys in Katutura Before

The Informant Sample

SCHEDULES AND questionnaires on a variety of subjects were used as a basic part of the study. Initially, it was attempted to survey households in Katutura, but I found this to be impossible. Informants were not at home, they were reluctant to answer questions, they were suspicious, or hostile. I decided that a number of informants from all ethnic and racial groups would be contacted through friends and research assistants, as would those with whom the fieldworker came into contact and who were amenable to answering questions. In this way, an opportunity informant sample of 150 people was compiled. In addition, data on household composition, conjugal unions, economics, and other data were based on large samples of the population from public records (see below).

The informant sample included informants' answers to open and closed questions. These data also include informants' verbal responses to questions, behavior responses which I was able to observe and record, and observations made during the course of the interviews. In some cases it was necessary to ask informants questions which required a yes or a no for an answer. On account of the fieldwork situation, the tendency was for people to answer these questions in the affirmative. In these cases, I asked a series of questions that allowed cross-checking of informants' responses. When it is appropriate to indicate the source of material drawn from the informant sample, this has been done. This material also provided an indispensable background for much of the qualitative description. In addition to the informant sample data, I collected a large amount of descriptive and observational data.

As in most anthropological fieldwork, an attempt was made to find informants who had that special talent for being able to explain and understand some of the reasons for their own and other people's behavior. There were ten such informants, with whom I talked at length about many topics. These informants, anthropologists of their own society, contributed many valuable observations and insights to this study. Discussions with informants took place in Afrikaans, German, and English. I cannot claim a fluent speaking knowledge of Afrikaans or German, but a working knowledge of both languages was achieved. Most people in the area had a speaking knowledge of at least one of these languages, usually Afrikaans, but research assistants acted as interpreters when necessary. Two research assistants often collected data on their own. I attempted to learn as much as possible about the languages used in Windhoek, but I did not achieve a speaking knowledge of any of them. Important words and phrases were learned and, where necessary, have been included in the text with English translations.

Windhoek Survey

During 1968 the Windhoek municipality employed a Johannesburg town-planning firm to assist the municipality in formulating a master plan for the future growth and development of the Windhoek Urban Area. Teams of interviewers using schedules talked to people in most white and coloured households in the Urban Area. These data were made available to me by the municipality, and some of this data has been used for background information and population statistics. A demographic study was also commissioned by the municipality; the results of this study were also made available to me.

Service Contract Survey

The registration office of the Windhoek Non-European Affairs Department kept a card on each nonwhite man who lived in

Katutura and was employed. During April 1968, these data were recorded by a research assistant. Information on the ethnic group, salary, place of origin or domicile, and classification of 4,355 men was obtained. These data represented nearly all employed black men in the Urban Area, with the exception of Owambo contract workers.

Katutura Housing Card Survey (Katutura Survey)

For each house in Katutura, there was a card on file in the Katutura housing office of the Windhoek Non-European Affairs Department. These cards contained the following information: type of conjugal union, ethnic group, sex, age, number of children, and relationship of the children to the household head. The same information was recorded for relatives and friends who lived in the house. The total number of households in the survey was 3,335, which represented about 95 percent of all the households in Katutura at the time of the survey. Five percent of the cards were eliminated owing to insufficient or inaccurate information. With the help of several assistants, these data were recorded on summary sheets in March and September 1968. The September data covered those blacks who moved to Katutura when the Old Location was closed. The March and September data do not overlap and were combined in the survey. I discussed my research with the black municipal clerks who conducted these surveys, explaining to them the importance of obtaining accurate information on the topics mentioned above, as well as how they should go about obtaining this information. A random check of 150 households indicated that the data collected were adequate for the purposes of this study.

Travel Pass Survey

The data on travel passes covers 1967. It was collected from the Department of Bantu Administration and Development in Windhoek. There were 2,670 travel passes containing the following information: sex, ethnic group, destination, name, and the period of time for which the pass was valid.

Visitors to Katutura and the Old Location

Data on visitors also covered 1967 and was a 3 percent sample of the approximately 13,000 visitors' permits issued.

Marriage Register Survey

Data for the Marriage Register Survey were taken from the official marriage register book in the Magistrate's Office, Windhoek, which was associated with the Department of Bantu Administration and Development, and from the records of the Lutheran and Roman Catholic Churches. Data were recorded for church and magistrate's marriages for each five-year period from 1935 to 1960 and for each year from 1965 to 1968. These data include only marriages that took place in Windhoek and involve primarily Windhoek residents.

Appendix 2

Details of Surveys Used in Katutura Now

Katutura Survey 1991 (KAT1991)

THE KATUTURA SURVEY was conducted in March 1991. The project was funded by the European Economic Community (EEC) and the Windhoek Municipality. Data were collected from a representative sample of people living in the twenty-three residential communities that make up Katutura (see Table 2). The sample consisted of survey interviews with people on 300 household sites. Some household sites had more than one family located on them, and the number of families interviewed came to 369. Data on 1,865 people were collected in the survey. Debie LeBeau organized data entry, cleanup, and the writing of analysis programs for the initial data analysis that was reported in Pendleton (1991). Subsequent data analysis was done by the author.

The number of housing sites (*erven*) in each of the various residential areas of Katutura was counted. The number of surveys to be conducted in each area was based on the percentage of household sites that that area contributed to the total number of household sites. For example, Wanaheda has 2,225 household sites, the total number of household sites in Katutura was estimated to be 11,610; therefore, Wanaheda makes up 19.1 percent of the household sites. A total of fifty-seven interviews or 19.1 percent of the 300 planned survey interviews were conducted in Wanaheda. The number of surveys to be conducted in each of the other Katutura areas was calculated in the same manner. See Table 2 for the number of surveys completed in each area of Katutura.

The sample interval was every thirty-eighth household site, established by dividing the number of planned surveys by the total number of household sites. Municipal maps of Katutura were used, and interviewers were given maps of the area where they were to work. Household sites were selected in the following manner: starting at the top upper left-hand corner of the map of the respective residential area, and moving from left to right across the map for that area and down the map as though it were a book, every thirty-eighth household site was identified for the survey.

Every effort was made to determine the number of households living at each dwelling site, and the head of each household was asked to provide information on all members of the household. Interviewers were chosen for each of the residential areas based on their knowledge of the area and their language fluency, since it was necessary at times to translate questions into the various ethnic languages. Each survey was checked for reliability and consistency by two field supervisors who were responsible for the survey research project. Data entry and data cleaning took place at NISER in March and April 1991. Data-cleaning programs were written to find data-entry errors and inconsistencies in the survey data. Debie LeBeau and I did the data analysis for the 1991 Katutura survey.

Household Health and Nutrition Survey (HHNS)

The questionnaire was administered by UNICEF and consists of several hundred questions relating to household and individual attributes, child health information, and female fertility data. UNICEF provided the primary funding for the project. Many questions in this survey are similar to those asked in the Nexus survey questionnaire; however, this database has much additional data obtained through measurements of children (Cogill and Kiugu 1990). The database contains questions on returnees, household, child health, and female fertility information. The focus of the original survey was the health and nutrition of women and children.

HHNS Sampling. This survey was based on a two-stage random stratified sample. Katutura was divided into two parts, the old and new Katutura, and each part was then further divided into subsections based on ethnicity. Household lists were obtained from the municipality, and households were randomly selected from these lists (Cogill and Kiugu 1990:128–132).

The dataset was provided by FSG Oxford, and Debie LeBeau organized and documented the dataset. LeBeau and Pendleton (1993A) report findings from the HHNS.

The Health and Daily Living Survey (HDL)

The HDL was conducted during three-month intervals in 1988 and 1989 in the Windhoek area, including Katutura, Khomasdal, and Windhoek. A total of 569 households selected in a systematic manner comprise the dataset. Topics included in the questionnaire were basic demographic data and cultural data, social functioning and resource indices, family functioning and home environment, substance use, psychosocial scales, health seeking behavior, children's health, and stress. The sampling for Katutura was similar to that described for the 1991 Katutura Survey. Results were published as Pendleton (1990b). The project received partial support from the University of Namibia, the Department of National Health and Welfare of the Government of Namibia, and the San Diego State University.

The NBC Radio Listeners Survey (RADIO)

This nation-wide study collected data on attitudes, preferences and needs relating to the Namibian radio service. The project was funded by UNESCO and the NBC. These data were collected from all areas and socioeconomic groups in Namibia. This survey identifies the number and gender of returnees in the household, and household/individual demographics. Questions on returnees were included in this survey to provide data for the Project. Results were published as Pendleton and LeBeau (1992).

Survey data for this study were collected from June to August 1992.

Approximately 200 households in each of the language/communal areas in the country were interviewed. Of those 200 interviews, forty were conducted in each district center, and 160 in each rural area. Two hundred interviews were conducted with commercial farm owners and farm workers, approximately 200 interviews in Windhoek, and 200 interviews were divided between four selected towns around the country.

RADIO Sampling. For the district centers, selected towns and Windhoek urban population figures were estimated from Frayne (1992:20–22) and used to develop a Nth sampling interval. The person in the selected household was chosen using a standard survey method. That enabled the respondent's age, gender, and working status to be varied.

War-Affected People Survey (WAP)

This is a demographic and attitudinal survey (N = 2,162) conducted in the Owambo Regions and Katutura in May and June 1992. Primary funding for the project was provided by the EEC. This database contains both household and individual information. Results were published as Preston et al. (1993). Pendleton supervised data collection for the project in Owambo, Rundu, Katima Mulilo, and Katutura, and did the data analysis for the community studies reported in the project document. LeBeau and Pendleton (1993b) wrote component 5b of the report, "Unpublished Information: Surveys and the Social and Economic Characteristics of Returnee and Stayer Groups," reported in Preston et al. (1993).

Energy Usage Survey (ENERGY)

This is an energy usage survey (N = 303) conducted in northern Namibia and Katutura between December 1991 and February 1992, and was sponsored by the World Bank. This database contains household information.

Appendix 3

Some Notes on Tables Used in the Text

1. Percentages and totals are for columns, unless noted otherwise.
2. Percentages do not always total 100 due to rounding.
3. Tables marked 1968 or 1969 are taken from the 1974 book.
4. Tables marked 1991 are from KAT1991.
5. Tables marked 1992 are from ENERGY.
6. Tables marked 1988 are from HDL.
7. Statistics used in the tables are mean, median, standard deviation.
8. All tables are listed in the table of contents under the list of tables.

Table 1: Offenses Committed by Africans in Urban Area (1969)

Offense	Number of Offenses	Fines (R)	Days in Jail
Rent due	443	3,466	6,292
In the location without permission	2,155	17,526	23,833
Providing illegal accommodation	381	1,114	803
Disturbance of the peace	37	187	285
Ownership of dangerous weapons	4	125	220
Urinating in a public place	101	313	306
Whites in location without permission	8	60	—
Absence from work	9	75	180
Unlawfully in South West Africa	2	—	—
Extra-territorial and northern section African illegally in the urban area	168	2,063	4,570
In town area longer than 72 hours without a pass	797	12,788	26,140
Possession of dagga (marijuana)	12	200	270
Transgressing registration laws	441	1,148	2,884
Unregistered person in house	43	201	340
Drunkenness	4	28	70
Forged documents	2	40	110
Failure to produce service contract	199	563	1,130
Failure to register	28	108	225
Illegal entry	55	175	375
Ignoring an order	2	10	40
Dirty area or yard	66	435	20
Receiving liquor	2	50	—
Hindering the police	2	25	140
Total	4,961	40,700	67,833

Source: Windhoek Annual Report 1969, Non-European Affairs Section, page 15.

Table 2. Number of People and Families per Dwelling Site (1991)

Katutura Area	Mean Number of People	Mean Number of Families	Number of Sites in Each Area	Number of People in Area	Number of Interviews Conducted
Bloedrivier	3.8750	2.5000	168	1.630	8
Damara I	5.6250	1.2500	280	1.971	8
Damara II	5.3571	1.5714	445	3.745	14
Damara III	5.9167	1.1667	871	5.992	24
Freedom Square	5.0000	1.0000	88	440	2
Gemengde	4.6667	2.1667	307	3.111	12
Golgotha	5.0000	2.1250	345	3.674	16
Grysblok	5.3333	1.0000	245	1.306	6
Hakahana	3.9565	1.1739	818	3.790	23
Herero I	4.6957	1.5217	707	5.051	23
Herero II	6.0000	1.0000	448	2.688	12
Luxury Hill	5.8889	1.2222	292	2.098	9
Marula	5.7500	1.0000	311	1.788	8
Nama	3.6364	1.7273	257	1.618	11
Okuryangava	3.2353	1.3529	525	2.296	17
Owambo I Donkerhoek	5.8000	1.1333	524	3.476	15
Owambo II	6.3750	1.2500	292	2.274	8
Police Camp	6.5000	1.0000	71	462	2
Shandumbala A	7.0000	1.0000	233	1.631	6
Shandumbala B	5.7143	1.5714	199	1.784	7
Single Quarters	4.1724	1.9310	150	1.207	29
Soweto	6.3529	1.0588	1.367	9.201	34
Wanaheda	4.7500	2.0395	2.225	21.560	75
Total	5.0459	1.5568	11.610	91.464	369

NOTE: The sample interval for the survey was 38, and 369 surveys were conducted. The total number of people was calculated by taking the mean number of people per family times the mean number of families per area times the number of sites per area.

Table 3: Population Gender (1991)

Gender	People	Percent
Male	986	53
Female	880	47
Total	1,866	100

Table 4: Population Age (1991)

	People	Mean	Median
Population age	1,867	24.16	23

Table 5: Population Ethnicity—Language (1991)

Language	People	Percent
Afrikaans	83	4
Caprivi	1	0
Damara	356	19
English	2	0
Herero	359	19
Kavango	4	0
Nama	179	10
Owambo	784	42
Other	96	5
Total	1,864	100

Table 6: Population Education Adults 16+ (1991)

Education Level	People	Percent
None	133	10
Sub A	30	2
Sub B	40	3
Std 1	56	4
Std 2	109	9
Std 3	86	7
Std 4	121	10
Std 5	133	10
Std 6	178	14
Std 7	112	9
Std 8	114	9
Std 9	34	3
Std 10	91	7
Std 10 + diploma	20	2
Std 10 + degree	8	1
Masters/Ph.D.	5	0
Total	1,270	100

Table 7: Population Literacy (1991)

	People	Percent
Read only	38	2
Write only	13	1
Read and write	1,417	77
Illiterate	168	9
Too young	215	12
Total	1,851	100

Table 8: Population Work Status (1991)

Work Status	People	Percent
Working	611	58
Not working	74	7
Seeking work	367	35
Total	1,052	100

Table 9: Personal Income (1991)

	People	Mean	Median	Std. Dev.
Personal income	612	606	500	543

Table 10: Population Occupation Excluding Unemployed (1991)

Occupation	People	Percent
Professional	61	10
Technical	33	5
Clerk	37	6
Skilled labor	95	16
Laborer	85	14
Civil servant	53	9
Sales representative	46	8
Service worker	111	18
Informal sector	89	15
Total	610	100

Table 11: Drinking of Alcohol by Demographics (1988)

Demographics	Drinking				Total	
	Yes		No		People	Percent
	People	Percent	People	Percent		
Education						
None	13	62	8	38	21	100
Less than Std 1	7	64	4	36	11	100
Std 1–4	15	39	23	61	38	100
Std 5–7	49	54	42	46	91	100
Std 8–10	42	49	43	51	85	100
College or technicon	18	56	14	44	32	100
University	6	55	5	45	11	100
Vocational	6	67	3	33	9	100
Religion						
Catholic	51	57	38	43	89	100
Dutch Reformed	1	20	4	80	5	100
Lutheran	71	52	65	48	136	100
Anglican	5	45	6	55	11	100
Methodist	10	56	8	44	18	100
Oruano	2	50	2	50	4	100
None	5	63	3	38	8	100
Other	10	38	16	62	26	100
Gender						
Male	91	58	66	42	157	100
Female	66	46	77	54	143	100
Katutura Development						
1950–80	98	52	90	48	188	100
1980–90	67	53	53	47	112	100
Household Income						
Below median	90	52	82	48	172	100
Above median	67	54	58	46	125	100
Household Type						
Conjugal	112	54	95	46	207	100
Female-centered	22	42	31	58	53	100
Male-centered	17	57	13	43	30	100

Table 12: Number of Days Alcoholic Beverages Consumed in One Week (1988)

Beverage	Less Than One		One to Two		Three to Seven	
	People	Percent	People	Percent	People	Percent
Wine	103	67	34	22	17	11
Bottled Brew	72	47	48	31	34	22
Hard liquor	115	74	27	17	13	8
Home brew	119	79	8	5	23	15

NOTE: Percentages total across rows.

Table 13: Ethnic and Racial Group Terms

Terms marked with an asterisk (*) are of a derisive nature, while the following notes translate terms in the table on the following page.

1. Infidel in Arabic
2. Red-necks
3. They dangle their genitals in the ocean by always having a foot in safe Britain.
4. Black people
5. Pale whites
6. Original name of the Korana people
7. Whites
8. Rough people
9. Protruding ears (praise name)
10. People who circumcise
11. Red people
12. People with peppercorn hair
13. To swing (swingers)
14. Local German for Germans from Germany
15. Black people
16. Useless refuse
17. Those who look to be whites
18. Yellow people
19. Those who shave knuckles of their cattle
20. Black strangers
21. Red outsiders (pariah)
22. Strangers with large buttocks
23. Orange River people
24. White and Damara/Herero ancestry
25. Those with shoes
26. Excrement people
27. People of the sea
28. Pollard (praise name)
29. People with a gap in their teeth
30. Blocked-ears people
31. Black people
32. Yellow people
33. Fawn
34. White
35. People you cannot understand
36. Himba of the Kaokoveld
37. Khoen people
38. Those who don't save anything
39. Cattle Dama (black people)

Ethnic and Racial Reference Group Category

Speaker's Ethnic Group	Blacks	Coloureds	Whites	Afrikaners	Damaras	English	Germans	Hereros	Namas	Owambos
Afrikaner	Inboorlinge *Kaffers[1] Swartes *Houtkoppe	Kleurlinge Basters	Blankes	Afrikaners	Damaras Klipkaffers	Rooinekke[2] *Souties[3]	Duitsers *Blackkoppe	Herero's	Namas *Hotnots Hottentotte	*Vambo's Wambo's
Coloured	*Kaffers Natives Blacks	Kleurlinge	Blankes Boere	Afrikaners *Japies *Boere	*Kaffers Damaras	Engelsmanne *Rooinekke	Duitsers	Herero's	Namas *Hotnots	*Vambo's Wambo's
Damara	ǂNukhoen[4]	Bastern ǀHaillhûn[5] !Goran[6]	ǀHûn[7]	Burn ǀKhoran[8]	ǂNukhoen Damaran	ǀApa|aon[2]	Duistern ǁGaputǂgaen[9]	Hereron *Tsoratamaǂgän[10]	ǀApakhoen[11] ǀGarudanan[12]	*ǀNapen[1]
English	Blacks Natives *Kaffirs	Coloureds	Whites	Boers Afrikaners *Crunchies *Rock-spiders	Damaras	English	*Jerries *Krauts	Hereros	Namas Hottentots	Owambos
German	Schwarze Eingeborene *Kaffern	Farbige Bastards	Weiße	Afrikaner *Buren *Japies *Schlappohren	Bergdamaras Damaras	Engländer	*Schneebantu Importierte[14]	Hereros	Namas Hottentotten	Ovambos
Herero	Ovazorondu[15]	•Ovikonde[16] Ozombahau-rumbu[17]	Ovirumbu[18] Ozombuhura-zonyu[19]	Ozomburu	*Ovazorotwa[20]	Ovaingirisa	Ovandoitji	Ovaherero	*Ovaseratwa[21] Ovatwa voma-tako[22]	Ovambo
Nama	ǂNkhoen[4]	!Garinin[23] ǀHûdaman[24]	ǀHûn[7]	ǀKhoran[8] *ǁHaroxan[25]	*Xaudaman[26]	ǀApalaon Hurinîn[27]	!Omkhoen[28] !Omlhun ǁGapuxaǂgaen[9]	Soaxa-am-nan[29] Gomadaman[39] Haidaman **ǂGin[30]	Naman ǀApakhoen[11]	ǀNapen[13]
Wambo (Kwany.)	Ovalaule[31]	Oohailumbu[32] Ovambabi[33]	Oilumbu[32] Ovatokele[34]	Ovangolo	Ovatakumi[35]	Ovainginisha	Ovandowishi	Ovashimba[36] Ovaherero	Ovakwena[37] Ovakwanghala[38]	Ovawambo

Table 14: Type of Housing by Old and New Katutura (1991)

Type of Housing	Katutura Development				Total	
	1950–80		1980–90		Houses	Percent
	Houses	Percent	Houses	Percent		
Rent a room	31	16	33	19	64	17
Rent from municipality	106	55	58	33	164	44
Rent house from private	23	12	55	31	78	21
Rent space outside	0	0	5	3	5	1
Own the house	31	16	26	15	57	15
No rent paid	1	1	0	0	1	0
Total	192	100	177	100	369	100

NOTE: Total rentals = room 17% + municipal 44% + space 21% = 82%.

Table 15: Housing Costs by Type of Housing (1991)

Type of Housing	Rent/Month Expenses			
	Houses	Mean	Median	Std. Dev.
Rent a room	60	85	60	73
Own the house	34	268	200	293
Rent from municipality	163	136	120	108
Rent house from private	64	160	140	128
Rent space outside	2	75	75	0

Table 16: Months on Dwelling Site (1991)

	Houses	Mean	Median	Std. Dev.
Months in this house	368	104	64	110

Table 17: Dwelling Comfort for Household (1988)

Attribute	Positive		In Between		Negative	
	Houses	Percent	Houses	Percent	Houses	Percent
Neat	192	64	63	21	47	16
Clean	201	67	58	19	42	14
Comfortable	147	49	87	29	67	22
Quiet	133	44	88	29	80	27
Light	165	55	60	20	74	25
Size	107	35	62	21	133	44
Safe	137	46	80	27	83	28
All attributes	166	56	78	27	50	17

NOTE: Percentages total across rows.

Table 18: African Church and Magistrate's Marriages (1933–68)

Years	Number of Church Marriages	Percentage Increase/Decrease Per Period of 4 Years	Number of Magistrate's Marriages	Percentage Increase/Decrease Per period of 4 Years
1933–36	39	—	17	—
1937–40	71	+82.1	80	+370.6
1941–44	83	+16.9	91	+13.8
1945–48	73	-12.1	75	-17.6
1949–52	72	-1.4	49	-34.7
1953–56	107	+48.6	49	0.0
1957–60	70	-34.6	207	+322.5
1961–64	128	+82.9	256	+23.7
1965–68	199	+55.5	155	-39.5

Source: Marriage Register and Church Records.

Table 19: Household Expenses (1967)

Expense Category	Cost (R)	Percent of Total
House rent	4	4
Food: 53 lbs maize-meal and 16 lbs meat	45	43
Clothes	20	19
Fuel: paraffin, wood, or electricity	8	7
Water	1	1
Cleaning materials: soap, washing-powder, toothpaste, etc.	6	6
Furniture	6	6
Bus fares	7	7
Food at work	3	3
Other expenses	4	4
Total budget	104	100

Table 20: Sources of Household Income (1991)

Source of Income	Houses	Percent
Formal sector	217	59
Informal sector	59	16
From other people	12	3
Other sources	52	14
Formal and informal	26	7
Total	366	100

Table 21: Family Income and Unemployment by Family Type (1991)

Family Type	Family Income/Month						
	Houses	Mean	Median	Mode	Std. Dev.	Min.	Max.
Nuclear	127	1,071	800	700	1,107	0	9,550
Extended	94	1,307	966	700	1,086	0	6,247
Female-centered	92	736	500	100	757	0	5,600
Male-centered	54	1,055	900	700	726	0	3,720
Total	369	1,047	800	700	989	0	9,550
Family Members Unemployed							
Nuclear	127	1	0.00	0.00	2.27	0.00	8.00
Extended	94	1	0.00	0.00	2.37	0.00	11.00
Female-centered	92	1	0.00	0.00	2.32	0.00	10.00
Male-centered	54	0	0.00	0.00	1.16	0.00	8.00

Table 22: Monthly Expense and Income (1991)

Expense	Percent	Houses	Mean	Median	Min.	Max.	Std. Dev.
Rent	21	369	126	100	0	1,400	144
Food	27	369	163	150	0	700	103
Clothes	14	369	84	50	0	1,000	124
Utilities	10	369	58	20	0	2,000	138
Transport	11	369	64	40	0	900	87
Medical	6	369	35	12	0	650	64
Alcohol	3	369	18	0	0	300	35
Cigarettes	2	369	11	0	0	200	25
Entertainment	3	369	15	0	0	400	35
Other	4	369	26	0	0	1,400	121
Total expenses	100	369	600	490	0	3,520	460
Family income	—	369	1,047	800	0	9,550	989

NOTE: Each individual expense is given as a percentage of the total monthly expenses.

Table 23: Monthly Expense and Income by Household Type (1991)

Expense	Nuclear			Extended			Female-centered			Male-centered		
	No.	Mean	Medn.	No.	Mean	Medn.	No.	Mean	Medn.	No.	Mean	Medn.
Rent	127	120	100	94	142	100	92	134	120	54	99	75
Food	127	183	150	94	180	200	92	126	100	54	148	135
Clothes	127	88	50	94	102	50	92	56	41	54	88	50
Utilities	127	56	20	94	78	30	92	40	10	54	57	6
Transport	127	64	50	94	70	45	92	43	20	54	89	40
Medical	127	29	10	94	50	25	92	26	10	54	35	12
Alcohol	127	18	0	94	22	10	92	5	0	54	36	20
Cigarettes	127	16	0	94	12	0	92	5	0	54	7	0
Entertainment	127	18	0	94	14	0	92	11	0	54	17	0
Other	127	23	0	94	37	0	92	28	0	54	14	0
Total	127	614	500	94	706	594	92	474	424	54	591	483
Income	127	1,071	800	94	1,307	966	92	736	500	54	1,055	900

Table 24: Monthly Expense and Income by Household Type (1991)

Expense	Nuclear				Extended				Female-centered				Male-centered			
	Below Median		Above Median		Below Median		Above Median		Below Median		Above Median		Below Median		Above Median	
	%	M	%	M	%	M	%	M	%	M	%	M	%	M	%	M
Rent	19	68	20	173	23	95	19	176	27	88	29	219	20	80	16	118
Food	36	127	27	240	32	135	23	211	28	92	25	190	27	111	24	183
Clothes	13	47	15	130	13	53	15	136	11	37	12	92	17	68	14	106
Utilities	7	26	10	86	6	26	13	114	9	28	8	63	11	46	9	66
Transport	9	33	11	96	10	40	10	91	9	28	10	72	11	47	17	128
Medical	5	16	5	42	6	27	7	66	6	20	5	38	4	17	7	53
Alcohol	4	14	3	22	4	17	3	25	1	2	2	11	7	28	6	44
Cigarettes	4	15	2	17	3	12	1	12	1	3	1	7	1	4	1	10
Entertainment	2	8	3	27	1	6	2	20	2	7	3	21	2	8	3	26
Other	1	4	5	43	3	11	6	56	6	20	6	42	1	2	3	25
Total	100	356	100	876	100	423	100	907	100	324	100	754	100	411	100	758
Income	—	456	—	1,695	—	471	—	1,899	—	341	—	1,478	—	500	—	1,570

NOTE: In this table, M = Mean

Table 25: Basic Food Items Consumed (1988)

Item	Daily		Weekly		Monthly		Never	
	House	Percent	House	Percent	House	Percent	House	Percent
Basic Products								
Maize-meal	187	62	85	28	28	9	1	0
Rice	42	14	169	56	67	22	23	8
Potatoes	57	19	154	52	63	21	25	8
Brown bread	201	67	74	25	19	6	8	3
White bread	23	8	118	39	75	25	85	28
Dairy Products	119	39	116	38	59	20	8	3
Meat Products								
Tripe	52	17	111	37	71	24	65	22
Beef	29	10	142	47	92	31	36	12
Mutton	33	11	118	39	111	37	38	13
Chicken	43	14	149	50	98	33	10	3
Fish	26	9	75	25	118	39	81	27
Canned meat	15	5	61	20	100	33	124	41
Vegetables								
Fresh vegetables	37	12	133	44	76	25	54	18
Canned vegetables	11	4	80	27	95	32	114	38
Fresh salads	17	6	113	38	101	34	69	23
Fresh fruit	42	14	104	35	89	30	63	21
Canned fruit	11	4	71	24	105	35	113	38

Table 26: Frequency of Alcoholic Beverages Consumed (1988)

Beverage	None		<1–2 / Week		3–4 / Week		Nearly Every Day	
	People	Percent	People	Percent	People	Percent	People	Percent
Wine	81	53	56	36	9	6	8	5
Bottled beer	33	21	87	56	22	14	12	8
Hard liquor	81	52	61	39	12	8	1	1
Home brew	115	77	12	8	4	3	19	13

Table 27: Frequency of Alcoholic Beverages Consumed by Household Income (1988)

Beverage	Household Below Median							
	None		<1–2 / Week		3–4 / Week		Nearly Every Day	
	People	Percent	People	Percent	People	Percent	People	Percent
Wine	41	46	37	41	6	7	6	7
Bottled beer	17	19	51	57	15	17	7	8
Hard liquor	52	58	30	33	8	9	0	0
Home brew	61	70	8	9	3	3	15	17
	Household Above Median							
Wine	40	63	19	30	3	5	2	3
Bottled beer	16	25	36	56	7	11	5	8
Hard liquor	29	45	31	48	4	6	1	2
Home brew	54	86	4	6	1	2	4	6

Table 28: Fuel Use in Katutura (1992)

Fuel	Never		Occasionally		Sometimes		Always	
	House	Percent	House	Percent	House	Percent	House	Percent
Firewood	23	22	46	45	20	20	13	13
Charcoal	93	91	5	5	4	4	0	0
Paraffin	88	85	4	4	9	9	2	2
Bottle-gas	68	66	12	12	19	19	4	4
Electricity	14	14	0	0	1	1	88	85

Table 29: Possessions in Katutura (1992)

Possession	Yes		No	
	Houses	Percent	Houses	Percent
Radio	86	83	17	17
Television	58	56	45	44
Stereo	37	36	66	64
Refrigerator	82	80	21	20
Gas stove	17	17	85	83
Electric stove	54	52	49	48
Iron	83	81	20	19
Hot plate	30	29	72	71
Electric kettle	55	54	47	46
Fan/Air conditioner	35	35	66	65
Electric heater	25	24	78	76
Torch	33	32	70	68
Vehicle	29	28	74	72

Table 30: Number of Family Problems in Katutura (1991)

Problem	Nuclear			Extended			Female-centered			Male-centered			Total		
	No.	M	Mdn.	No.	M	Mdn.	No.	M	Mdn.	No.	M	Mdn.	No.	M	Mdn.
Health	126	2	2	92	3	3	91	3	2	54	2	2	365	3	2
Crime	126	2	2	93	2	2	92	2	2	54	3	3	367	2	2
Children	127	3	2	93	2	2	91	3	3	53	2	2	366	2	2
Food	126	4	5	93	4	5	90	4	4	54	4	4	365	4	5
Education	127	3	3	93	3	3	91	3	3	54	3	4	366	3	3
Money	127	4	5	93	4	5	89	4	5	54	4	5	365	4	5
Housing	127	4	5	93	4	4	90	4	4	54	4	5	366	4	5
Employment	123	4	4	93	4	5	92	4	4	54	4	5	364	4	4
Domestic	125	2	2	91	2	2	90	2	2	52	2	2	360	2	2

NOTE: In this table, M = Mean and Mdn. = Median.

Table 31: Who Solves Family Problems (1991)

	People	Percent
Can you overcome the most serious problem?		
Yes	157	43
No	117	32
Maybe	88	25
Total	362	100
Who should solve your problems?		
Yourself	135	38
Family and friends	19	4
Local community efforts	11	3
Local community and government	49	14
Government	142	40
Other	4	1
Total	360	100

Table 32: Family Problems by Who Solves Them (1991)

	Total Number of Problems		
	People	Mean	Median
Can you overcome the most serious problem?			
Yes	144	3.4	3.6
No	107	3.1	3.1
Maybe	84	3.1	3.1
Total	335	3.2	3.3
Who should solve your problems?			
Yourself	126	3.6	3.7
Family and friends	19	3.1	3.2
Local community efforts	8	2.8	2.8
Local community and government	47	3.0	3.0
Government	129	3.0	3.0
Other	4	3.3	3.3
Total	333	3.2	3.3

Table 33: Average Annual Percentage Growth of Windhoek (Before)

Years	Africans[1]	Africans[2]	Coloureds	Whites
1921–36	-0.9%	-0.9%	+28.7%	+2.6%
1936–46	+3.3%	+4.6%	-0.7%	+4.5%
1946–51	+5.7%	+7.6%	-2.1%	+9.5%
1951–60	+3.6%	+5.9%	+14.1%	+9.7%
1960–68	+6.1%	+5.9%	+19.2%	+3.9%
1968–70	+14.6%	+12.3%	+10.3%	+4.2%

[1] Does not include any Owambo contract workers in the calculations

[2] Includes Owambo contract workers

Source: Official population census and Windhoek Survey.

Table 34: Windhoek Population (Before)

Years	Africans[1]	Coloureds	Whites	Total
1893	300–600	—	160	700
1903	1,935	119	610	3,324
1912	4,126	59	2,861*	7,046
1921	—	273	3,460	—
1927	4,757	—	—	—
1936	4,385	1,454	4,812	10,651
1946	6,591	1,353	6,985	14,929
1951	9,080	1,208	10,310	20,598
1960	13,935	2,738	19,378	36,051
1968	20,461	6,947	25,417	52,825
1970	25,464	8,376	27,529	61,369

[1] Includes Owambo contract workers.

* The 1913 figure for whites includes army personnel.

Source: Official population census, Bley 1971:77–78, Mossolow 1965:136.

Table 35: Place of Origin of Katutura Men (Before)

Ethnic Group	Windhoek	SWA Towns	Farm	Owambo	Herero Reserve	Other Reserve	Outside SWA	Total
Angola*	5	13	—	10	—	—	22	50
Bechuana	38	68	3	—	96	—	5	210
Damara	826	572	85	2	9	47	3	1,544
Herero	512	286	20	2	447	7	5	1,279
Nama	111	237	27	1	2	1	1	380
Town Owambo**	222	198	7	186	5	1	12	631
Other***	16	20	1	1	337	—	62	133
Total	1,730	1,394	143	202	592	56	110	4,227

* Angola includes African ethnic groups from Angola.

** Contract Owambo are not included, since their place of origin is Owambo.

*** Includes ethnic groups from outside South West Africa, e.g., Xhosa.

Source: Service Contract Survey.

Table 36: Why Adults Left Rural Areas (1991)

Reason	People	Percent
No money	306	32
No jobs	360	37
Poor schools	71	7
Poor hospitals	9	1
Poor social life	49	5
Don't like farming	6	1
No university	1	0
Pregnancy	13	1
Other	146	15
Total	961	100

Table 37: Why Adults Left Other Areas by Gender (1991)

Reason	Male		Female	
	People	Percent	People	Percent
No money	211	38	95	24
No jobs	241	43	119	30
Poor schools	30	5	41	10
Poor hospitals	2	0	7	2
Poor social life	24	4	25	6
Don't like farming	3	1	3	1
No university	0	0	1	0
Pregnancy	0	0	13	3
Other	51	9	94	24
Total	562	100	398	100

Table 38: Why Adults Left Other Areas by Previous Residence (1991)

Reason	Commercial Farm		Town		Communal Area		Other	
	People	Percent	People	Percent	People	Percent	People	Percent
No money	3	10	32	23	245	36	26	22
No jobs	8	26	50	35	277	41	25	22
Poor schools	12	39	17	12	40	6	2	2
Poor hospitals	1	3	3	2	5	1	0	0
Poor social life	3	10	6	4	37	5	3	3
Don't like farming	1	3	1	1	4	1	0	0
No university	0	0	0	0	1	0	0	0
Pregnancy	0	0	4	3	7	1	2	2
Other	3	10	28	20	57	8	58	50
Total	31	100	141	100	673	100	116	100

Table 39: Push/Pull Factors of Migration (1991)

	People	Percent
Reason for leaving rural areas		
No money	305	32
No jobs	360	38
Poor schools	65	7
Poor social life	49	5
Other	171	18
Total	950	100
Reason for coming to Katutura		
Job/money	685	72
School/education	87	9
Other	186	19
Total	958	100

Table 40: Factors Associated with Ties to Rural Areas (1991)

	People	Percent
What is kept in rural areas		
Fields	56	6
Livestock	103	10
Both	148	15
Nothing	681	69
Total	988	100
Is money sent outside WIndhoek		
Yes, regularly	133	13
No	576	58
Sometimes	286	29
Total	995	100
Where is the money sent?		
Commercial farm	11	3
Other town	27	7
Owambo	264	63
Kaokoland	4	1
Kavango	4	1
Caprivi	1	0
Damaraland	38	9
Hereroland	31	7
Namaland	18	4
Other	19	5
Total	417	100

Table 41: First Residence After Arrival in Katutura (1991)

Residence	People	Percent
Family	582	59
Friends	200	20
On your own	99	10
Other	105	11
Total	986	100

Table 42: Alternatives in the Event of Things Going Wrong (1991)

Alternative	People	Percent
Return to previous residence	463	46
Move to another area	194	20
Stay in Windhoek	335	34
Total	992	100

Table 43: Language Group by Years in Katutura (1991)

Language Group	0.1–2 Years		2.1–5 Years		5.1–12 Years		12.1 Years +		Total	
	N	%	N	%	N	%	N	%	N	%
Herero	37	24	33	21	35	22	52	33	157	16
Nama	9	12	12	15	24	31	33	42	78	8
Damara	21	18	25	22	15	13	55	47	116	12
Owambo	199	34	145	25	132	23	102	18	578	58
Afrikaans	7	26	3	11	9	33	8	30	27	3
Other	10	22	9	20	13	28	14	30	46	5
Total	283	28	227	23	228	23	264	26	1,002	100

NOTE: Percentages total across rows.

Table 44: Skills by Years in Katutura (1991)

Skills	0.1–2 Years		2.1–5 Years		5.1–12 Years		12.1 Years +		Total	
	N	%	N	%	N	%	N	%	N	%
Building industry	6	16	13	35	5	14	13	35	37	4
Automobile industry	4	27	5	33	2	13	4	27	15	2
Plumber	6	18	15	46	5	15	7	21	33	3
Welder	10	36	6	21	9	32	3	11	28	3
Electrician	4	14	8	28	10	35	7	24	29	3
Cook	15	17	21	24	19	22	31	36	86	9
Sewing	9	19	12	25	11	23	16	33	48	5
Unskilled	129	39	66	20	62	19	70	21	327	34
Other	84	23	76	21	95	26	105	29	360	37
Total	267	28	222	23	218	23	256	27	963	100

NOTE: Percentages total across rows.

Table 45: Occupation by Years in Katutura (1991)

Occupation	0.1–2 Years		2.1–5 Years		5.1–12 Years		12.1 Years +		Total	
	N	%	N	%	N	%	N	%	N	%
Professional	19	35	10	19	12	22	13	24	54	6
Technical	9	29	10	32	3	10	9	29	31	3
Clerk	3	10	5	17	12	40	10	33	30	3
Skilled worker	11	14	10	13	29	36	30	38	80	9
Laborer	11	15	23	30	16	21	26	34	76	8
Civil servant	6	16	14	37	7	18	11	29	38	4
Sales	8	19	13	30	8	19	14	33	43	4
Service worker	18	20	26	28	22	24	26	28	92	10
Wife/retired	5	10	8	16	12	24	25	50	50	6
Informal employment	15	18	26	31	21	25	22	26	84	9
Unemployed	146	43	64	19	68	20	60	18	338	37
Total	251	27	209	23	210	23	246	27	916	100

NOTE: Percentages total across rows.

Table 46: Dwelling Comfort for Old and New Katutura (1988)

Attribute	Positive		In Between		Negative	
	Houses	Percent	Houses	Percent	Houses	Percent
1950–80						
Neat	121	64	46	24	23	12
Clean	128	67	43	23	19	10
Comfortable	90	47	54	28	46	24
Quiet	77	41	58	31	54	29
Light	96	51	41	22	50	27
Size	71	37	39	21	80	42
Safe	85	45	54	29	50	26
All attributes	103	56	52	28	30	16
1980–90						
Neat	71	63	17	15	24	21
Clean	73	66	15	14	23	21
Comfortable	57	51	33	30	21	19
Quiet	56	50	30	27	26	23
Light	69	62	19	17	24	21
Size	36	32	23	21	53	47
Safe	52	47	26	23	33	30
All attributes	63	58	26	24	20	18

NOTE: Percentages total across rows.

Table 47: Type of Housing for Old and New Katutura (1991)

Type of Housing	1950–80		1980–90	
	Houses	Percent	Houses	Percent
Rent a room	31	16	33	19
Rent from municipality	106	55	58	33
Rent house from private	23	12	55	31
Rent space outside	0	0	5	3
Own the house	31	16	26	15
No rent paid	1	1	0	0
Total	192	100	177	100

Table 48: Population Income (1991)

	1950–80	1980–90
Houses	334	345
Median	503	630
Mean	400	500

Table 49: Frequency of Alcoholic Beverages Consumed(1988)

Beverage	Old Katutura							
	None		<1–2 / Week		3–4 / Week		Nearly Every Day	
	People	Percent	People	Percent	People	Percent	People	Percent
Wine	29	43	29	43	4	6	6	9
Bottled beer	18	27	32	47	11	16	7	10
Hard liquor	39	57	22	32	7	10	0	0
Home brew	45	68	7	11	1	2	13	20
	New Katutura							
Wine	51	60	27	32	5	6	2	2
Bottled beer	14	17	55	65	11	13	5	6
Hard liquor	41	47	39	45	5	6	1	1
Home brew	69	83	5	6	3	4	16	17

Table 50: Family Income by Household Type (1991)

Household Type	Family Income/Month						
	Houses	Mean	Median	Mode	Std. Dev.	Min.	Max.
Below							
Nuclear	58	421	425	700	201	0	700
Extended	36	444	489	700	236	0	750
Female-centered	55	299	265	100	186	0	780
Male-centered	24	475	528	700	251	0	760
Above							
Nuclear	68	1,695	1,380	1,000	1,287	845	9,550
Extended	55	1,899	1,710	1,400	1,062	850	6,247
Female-centered	32	1,478	1,302	1,000	846	803	5,600
Male-centered	28	1,570	1,425	1,350	635	900	3,720

Table 51: Type of Housing by Household Income (1991)

Type of Housing	Household Income				Total	
	Below Median		Above Median		Houses	Percent
	Houses	Percent	Houses	Percent		
Rent a room	42	22	22	12	64	17
Own the house	27	14	30	16	57	15
Rent from municipality	65	35	99	54	164	44
Rent house from private	49	26	29	16	78	21
Rent space outside	3	2	2	1	5	1
No rent paid	1	1	0	0	1	0
Total	187	100	182	100	369	100

Table 52: Frequency of Alcoholic Beverages
Consumed by Household Income (1988)

Beverage	< Once to None		Once or Twice		3–7 Times	
	People	Percent	People	Percent	People	Percent
Below						
Wine	53	59	25	28	12	13
Bottled Brew	44	49	24	27	22	24
Hard liquor	69	77	13	14	8	9
Home brew	63	72	6	7	18	21
Above						
Wine	50	78	9	14	5	8
Bottled Brew	28	44	24	38	12	19
Hard liquor	46	71	14	22	5	8
Home brew	56	89	2	3	5	8

References Cited

Banghart, P. 1969. *A Study of Migrant Labour in South West Africa and Its Effects on Ovambo Tribal Life.* M.A., Stellenbosch University.

Beining, E. 1988. "Ein 'Schandfleck' wird ausgemerzt." In H. Melber (ed), *Katutura—Ghetto im Alltag.* Bonn: Informationsstelle Südliches Afrika e.V. (issa).

Berreman, G.D. 1964. The Aleut Reference Group Alienation, Mobility and Acculturation. *American Anthropologist* 66:231–250.

Bley, H. 1971. *South West Africa under German Rule 1884–1914.* London: Heineman (translation of 1968 German edition).

Boonzaier, E., and J. Sharp. 1988. *South African Keywords: The Uses and Abuses of Political Concepts.* Cape Town: David Philip.

Botelle 1992. *Onaanda Community-Based Road Construction Project, Western Owambo Region.* Windhoek: Namibian Institute for Social and Economic Research, Research Report No. 9.

Breitborde, L. 1994. "Urban Anthropology in the 1990s: W(h)ither the City? An Introduction." City and Society, Annual Review.

Cogill, B. and S. Kiugu. 1990. "Report on a Survey of Household Health and Nutrition in Katutura and Selected Northern Areas of Namibia." Windhoek: UNICEF and Ministry of Health and Social Services.

Ferguson, J. 1990. "Mobil Workers, Modernist Narratives: A Critique of the Historiography of Transition on the Zambian Copperbelt." *J.S. Afr. Studies* 16(3):3–85-412, 16(4): 603–621.

———. 1992. "The Country and the City on the Copperbelt." *Cultural Anthropology* 7(1):80–92.

Fosse, L. 1992. *The Social Construction of Ethnicity and Nationalism in Independent Namibia.* Namibian Institute for Social and Economic Research, Discussion Paper No. 14, Windhoek.

François, C. von. 1899. *Deutsch-Südwestafrika 1884–1893.* Berlin: Dietrich Reimer.

Frayne, B. 1992. *Urbanisation in Post-Independence Windhoek*. Windhoek: Namibian Institute for Social and Economic Research, Research Report No. 6.

Garnier, C. von (ed). 1986. *Katutura Revisited*. Windhoek: Angelus Printing.

Gibson, D. 1991. "Changes in the Position of Matrilineal Oshiwambo-Speaking Women in Katutura, Namibia." Unpublished seminar paper. Cape Town: University of Cape Town, Social Anthropology Seminar.

Goldblatt, I. 1971. *History of South West Africa*. Cape Town: Juta.

Gordon, R. 1990. "The Field Researcher as a Deviant: A Namibian Study." In P. Hugo (ed), *Truth Be in the Field*. Pretoria: University of South Africa.

———. 1992. *The Bushman Myth*. Boulder: Westview Press.

Gordon R., and A. Spiegel. 1993. "Southern Africa Revisited." In B. Siegal, A. Beals, and S. Tylor (eds), *Annual Reviews of Anthropology*. Palo Alto: Annual Reviews Inc.

Grotpeter, J. 1994. *Historical Dictionary of Namibia*. Metuchen, N.J. and London: The Scarecrow Press.

Hall, C. 1961. "Report of the Commission of Enquiry into the Occurrences in the Windhoek Location on the Night of the 10th and 11th December, 1959, and into the Direct Causes Which Led to Those Occurrences." Windhoek: Commission of Enquiry.

Hammersley, M. 1992. *What's Wrong with Ethnography?* London: Routledge.

Harries-Jones, P. 1969. "Home-Boy Ties and Political Organization in a Copperbelt Township." In J. Mitchell (ed), *Social Networks in Urban Situations*. Manchester: Manchester University Press.

Hintrager, O. 1955. *Südwestafrika in der deutschen Zeit*. München: Oldenbourg.

Hishongwa, N. 1992. *The Contract Labour System and Its Effects on Family and Social Life in Namibia*. Windhoek: Gamsberg Macmillan.

Iken, A., D. LeBeau, M. Menjengua, and W. Pendleton. 1994. *Socio-Economic Survey Eastern Communal Areas*. Windhoek: Directorate of Extension and Engineering, Ministry of Agriculture, Water, and Rural Development and Social Science Division, Multidisciplinary Research Centre, University of Namibia.

Jones, S. 1992. "Children on the Move: Parenting, Mobility, and Birth-Status among Migrants." In S. Burman and E. Preston-Whyte (eds), *Questionable Issue: Illegitimacy in South Africa*. Cape Town: Oxford University Press.

Kaakunga, E. 1990. *Problems of Capitalist Development in Namibia: The Dialectics of Progress and Destruction*. Aabo: Aabo Academic Press.

Kandetu, B. 1987. "Cultural Considerations for Namibia: Some Aspects." In G. Tötemeyer (ed), *Namibia in Perspective*. Windhoek: CCN.

Kandovazu, E. 1968. *Die Oruuano-Beweging*. Karibib: Rynse Sending-Drukkery.

Kangueehi, S. 1986. "From the 'Old Location' to Katutura." In C. von Garnier, *Katutura Revisited.* Windhoek: Angelus Printing.

Katjiuanjo, P., et al. 1993. *Namibia Demographic and Health Survey 1993.* Windhoek: Ministry and Health and Social Services, and Columbia, Maryland: Macro International.

Kiernan, J. 1990. *The Production and Management of Therapeutic Power in Zionist Churches within a Zulu City.* Lewiston: Mellon.

Köhler, O. 1959. *A Study of Grootfontein District* (South West Africa). Ethnological Publication No. 45. Pretoria: Government Printer.

———. 1960. *Sprachakkulturation im Herero.* Ethnologica (n.f.) 2:331–362.

Kotzé, C. 1990. *A Social History of Windhoek.* Ph.D., University of South Africa.

Lau, B. 1987. *Namibia in Jonker Afrikaner's Time.* Windhoek: National Archives.

———. 1988. "Pre-Colonial Namibian Historiography: What is to be Done." In: B. Wood (ed), *Namibia 1884–1984.* London: Namibia Support Committee.

———. 1991. *Namibia: Ethnic Stereotyping in a Post-apartheid State.* Windhoek: Namibian Institute for Social and Economic Research, Research Report No. 5.

———. 1993. *Phase I of Educationally Marginalised Children's Project: Baseline Desk Study.* A consultancy report prepared for the Ministry of Education and Culture. Windhoek: Namibian Institute for Social and Economic Research.

LeBeau, D. and W. Pendleton. 1993 A. *A Socio-Economic and Baseline Desk-Top Study of Health, Water, and Sanitation.* Windhoek: A consultancy report prepared for the Namibian Institute for Social and Economic Research.

———. 1993B. "Unpublished Information: Surveys and the Social and Economic Characteristics of Returnee and Stayer Groups." In Preston, M., et al. *The Integration of Returned Exiles, Former Combatants and Other War-Affected Namibians.* Windhoek: NISER.

Lee, R. 1993. *The Dobe Ju/'hoansi.* Second edition. New York: Harcourt Brace College Publishers.

Lemon, A. 1991. "The Apartheid City." In *Homes Apart.* Cape Town: David Philip.

Lewis, P. 1966. *The Creation of Soweto.* Non-European Affairs Department, Johannesburg City Council.

Lush, D. 1993. *Last Steps to Uhuru.* Windhoek: New Namibia Books.

Manona, C. 1991. "Relying on Kin." In A. Spiegel and P. McAllister (eds), *Tradition and Transition in Southern Africa.* Johannesburg: Witwatersrand University Press.

Mayer, P. 1961. *Townsmen or Tribesmen.* Cape Town: Oxford University Press.

Melber, H. 1985. "Stammeskulturen als Zivilisationsgut." In *Peripherie* (Berlin) 5 (18–19):143–61.

Melber, H. (ed). 1988. *Katutura—Ghetto im Alltag*. Bonn: Informationsstelle Südliches Afrika e.V. (issa).

———. 1988. "Hier haben wir eine Bleibe." In H. Melber (ed), *Katutura— Ghetto im Alltag*. Bonn: Informationsstelle Südliches Afrika e.V. (issa).

Mitchell, J. 1966. "Theoretical Orientations in African Urban Studies." In M. Banton (ed), *The Social Anthropology of Complex Societies*. London: Tavistock.

Moore, S. 1994. *Anthropology and Africa*. Charlottesville: University Press of Virginia.

Mossolow, N. 1965. *This Was Old Windhoek*. Windhoek: John Meinert.

Norval, D. and R. Namoya. 1992. *The Informal Sector within Greater Windhoek*. Windhoek: FNDC.

Pendleton, W. 1974. *Katutura: A Place Where We Do Not Stay*. San Diego: San Diego State University Press.

———. 1990A. "Fieldwork in Katutura, Namibia: Two Different Research Experiences." In Pierre Hugo (ed), *Truth Be in the Field*. Pretoria: University of South Africa.

———. 1990B. *Health and Daily Living Survey of Windhoek Namibia (1988–1989)*. Windhoek: Namibian Institute for Social and Economic Research, Research Report No. 2.

———. 1991. *The 1991 Katutura Survey Report*. Windhoek: Namibian Institute for Social and Economic Research, Discussion Paper No. 9.

Pendleton, W. and D. LeBeau. 1992. *Socio-Economic Analysis of Radio Listener Attitudes in Namibia*. A consultancy report prepared for the Namibian Broadcasting Corporation. Windhoek: Namibian Institute of Social and Economic Research, An Institute of the University of Namibia.

Pendleton, W., D. LeBeau, and C. Tapscott. 1992. *Socio-Economic Study of the Ondangwa/Oshakati Nexus Area*. Windhoek: Namibian Institute for Social and Economic Research, Research Report No. 8.

Poewe, C. 1985. *The Namibian Herero*. Lewiston/Queenston: Edwin Mellen Press.

Pool. G. 1991. *Samuel Maharero*. Windhoek: Gamsberg Macmillan.

Potgieter, J. n.d. "Background and Interpretation of the Household Subsistence Level." Port Elizabeth: Institute for Planning Research, University of Port Elizabeth.

Preston, R., et al. 1993. *The Integration of Returned Exiles, Former Combatants and Other War-Affected Namibians*. Windhoek, Namibian Institute for Social and Economic Research.

Reynolds, P. 1989. *Children in Crossroads: Cognition and Society in South Africa*. Cape Town: David Philip.

Ridgway, D., et al. 1991. *An Investigation of the Shooting at the Old Location on 10 December 1959. Discourse 2*. Windhoek: University of Namibia.

Scrimshaw, S. 1993. "Rapid Anthropological Assessment Procedures." In J. von Braun and D. Pütz (ed), *Data Needs for Food Policy in Developing Countries*. Washington: International Food Policy Research Institute.

Simon, D. 1991. "Windhoek: Desegregation and Change in the Capital of South Africa's Erstwhile Colony." In A. Lemon (ed), *Homes Apart*. Cape Town: David Philip.

Smith, D. 1992. "Conclusion." In D. Smith (ed), *The Apartheid City and Beyond*.

Sparks, D. and D. Green. 1992. *Namibia: The Nation After Independence*. Boulder: Westview Press.

Strauss, A. 1986. "Community Based Organisations (CBOs) in Katutura." In C. von Garnier (ed), *Katutura Revisited*. Windhoek: Angelus Printing.

Sundkler, B. 1961. *Bantu Prophets in South Africa*. New York: Oxford University Press.

Tapscott, C. 1993. "After Apartheid and After the War-Class Formation in Independent Namibia." In *The Two-Edged Sword: Namibia's Independence and Its Aftermath*. Athens: Ohio University Press.

Tapscott, C., and B. Mulongeni. 1990. *An Evaluation of the Welfare and Future Prospects of Repatriated Namibians in Northern Namibia*. Windhoek: Namibian Institute for Social and Economic Research, Discussion Paper No. 9.

Titus, S., and M. Goraseb. 1993. *Report HIV Infection 1992: Republic of Namibia*. Ministry of Health of Social Services, Epidemiology Section (unpublished).

Tuupainen, M. 1968. *Marriage in a Matrilineal African Tribe*. Helsinki: University of Helsinki.

van der Vliet, V. 1991. "Traditional Husbands, Modern Wives?" In A. Pigel and P. McAllister (eds), *Tradition and Transition in Southern Africa*. Johannesburg: Witwatersrand University Press.

Vaughn, D. 1993. "The African State and Indigenous Land Tenure: Ownership and Control of Communal Land in Namibia." M.A., University of Vermont.

Venter, A. 1967. "Plaaslike Nie-Bantu Werknemers." A memorandum prepared for the Windhoek City Council steering committee meeting of September 18, 1967.

Voipio, R. 1972. *Kontrak soos die Owambo dit sien*. Johannesburg: Christian Institute of Southern Africa.

Wagner, G. 1951. *Ethnographic Survey of South West Africa*. Unpublished manuscript found in the Offices of the Department of Bantu Administration and Development, Ethnological Section, Windhoek and used with permission. A copy of this manuscript has been placed in the National Archives by the author.

West, M. 1971. *Divided Community*. Cape Town: Balkema.

West, M. 1987. *Apartheid in a South African Town, 1968–1985*. Berkeley: Institute of International Studies, University of California.

Wilson, F., and M. Ramphele. 1989. *Uprooting Poverty: The South African Challenge*. Cape Town: David Philip.

Wilson, M., and A. Mafeje. 1963. *Langa*. Cape Town: Oxford University Press.

Ya-Otto, J. 1981. *Battlefront Namibia*. Westport: Lawrence Hill and Company.

Yaron, G., G. Janssen, and U. Maamberua. 1992. *Rural Development in the Okavango Region of Namibia*.Windhoek: Gamsberg Macmillan.

Index

Advisory Board: Katutura, 30, 31, 43–46, 47, 89, 96; Khomasdal, 46; Main Location, 28, 30

African: Advisory Board, 89; African Methodist Episcopal Church, 70; Anthropology, 5, 7; businesspeople, 111; clothing, 94; colonialism, 1; control of, 18; drinking of alcoholic beverages, 73; employment, 71, 133, 151; history in town, 2; housing tradition, 59; languages, 96, 97, 99; marriage, 117, 118, 121, 129; music, 85, 86; passbook problems, 32; population defined, 3; resentment of South African government, 11; wars fought with, 24–26, women in Windhoek, 40

Afrikaans, 16, 26, 38, 44, 46, 51, 69, 74, 82, 96, 97, 99, 101, 124, 126, 174

Afrikaner, 3, 22–24, 71, 95, 96, 97, 98, 100, 104

alcohol, 28, 72, 73–76, 103, 138, 139, 161, 163, 167

Angola, 18, 20, 31, 82, 152, 169

anthropology, 5, 6, 7, 9, 78

apartheid: abolished, 1, 54; Advisory Boards, 31; boundaries, 38; changes after, 55–57, 140, 165–169; chiefs, 29; churches, 70; cities, 40; during and after, 2; education, 51, 52, 95; employ-ment, 133, 134; enforcement, 38; housing, 111, 160; Katutura, 30; life under, 11; migration, 92, 149, 150; old Katutura, 14; paternalism, 71; policies, 39; racial terms of, 3; returnees, 81; stratification, 13, 99, 100, 157, 158; temporary migrants, 68; urban structure, 23

beer, 62

beerhall, 29, 41, 73–75, 85, 92; buying, 73; frequency of drinking, 75, 139, 162, 167; migrants, 91, 92; selling, 73, 133; shebeens, 74–75, 90

Botswana, 20, 25

bride price, 122, 124–128

Cape Town, 91, 168

church, 12, 33, 59, 70, 88, 100, 102, 103, 114–127, 129, 176

Clemens Kapuuo, 11, 31

coloured: Advisory Board, 49; Afrikaans, 38, 96, 97, 99; defined, 3; description, 93; drinking and smoking, 75; education, 51, 52; employment, 71; interaction, 100–102; Khomasdal, 40; Main Location, 28; moving out, 55; Nama, 95; regulations, 49; separate facilities, 38; South African Government, 43; stereotypes, 98,

99, 100; urban material culture, 42; Windhoek Survey, 174

communal area: bride price in, 125; Caprivi, 20; circumcision in, 94; closing of Old Location, 30; description, 18, 19, 90; development, 19; Eastern, 21; migration from, 23, 81, 150–153; NBC, 180; Okavango, 19, 20; Owambo, 19; Southern, 22, 81; survey attitudes, 13

compound (contract labor), 28, 30, 38, 53, 54, 57, 68, 91, 111, 113, 153, 154

conjugal, 14, 114–119, 122, 124–130, 132, 134, 137, 139, 161–164, 173, 175

contract workers, 28, 30, 40, 44, 47, 48, 91–93, 96, 151, 175

Damara: Advisory Board, 28, 43, 45; beerhall, 92; bride price, 122; church, 70; conjugal unions and marriage, 118, 125–127, 129; dancing, 86; description, 21, 84, 93, 94, 123; employment, 71; ethnic section, 49; farm workers, 21; female-centered, 161; house decorations, 42, 112; house numbers, 112; Katutura, 68, 69, 160; language, 21, 90, 92, 97; Old Location protests, 30; removal from Katutura, 43; school, 51; stereotypes, 95, 96, 98; team, 87; Windhoek migration, 24–26

Data Set, 10, 129, 179; ENERGY, 141, 180; HDL, 10, 13, 15, 75, 76, 98, 113, 138, 139, 141, 143, 179; HHNS, 10, 76, 104, 143, 178, 179; KATl991, 10, 72, 137, 140, 143, 177; RADIO, 10, 104, 179, 180; WAP, 10, 82, 104, 180

Department of Bantu Administration and Development, 43, 47, 175, 176

DTA, 31, 61, 103, 104

education (*see also* school), 160, 162, 163; Advisory Board, 28, 44; African Improvement Society,

30; Bantu Education, 51; bride price, 122; child nutrition, 77; communal area, 18; disparity in education, 71; drinking, 75, 76; employment, 132; household heads and members, 83, 162, 163; improvement, 56, 87; income, 163; levels in Katutura, 69, 160; marginalized, 56; migration, 149, 150, 152, 155, 156; Nama, 95; number of students, 52; Okavango, 20; problems, 140; returnees, 82; stereotypes, 88, 89, 98

elite, 28, 46, 88–90, 92, 158, l59

English, 12, 38, 46, 51, 69, 74, 79, 82, 86, 96–99, 104, 174

ethnic: association, 86, 87; boundaries, 7; categories, 88, 92, 93, 94, 167; communities, 26; homogeneity, 14, 50, 167; housing, 50; identity, 3, 7, 50, 167; Katutura demographic feature, 67–69, 83; schooling, 51; sections, 14, 26, 49, 53; segregation 50; stereotyping, 7, 71, 98

ethnic group: Advisory Board, 28, 43; brass bands, 30; characteristics, 94; conjugal unions and marriage, 117, 118, 123, 124, 128, 129, 130; households, 161; identity, 157, 158; Katutura composition, 69, 160; Kavango, 19; language, 21, 96, 97; meals, 9; migrants, 155; on surveys, 173, 175, 178, 179; place of origin, 151; sections, 38, 40, 50, 111; stereotypes, 95–97; terms, 99

ethnicity: African anthropology, 7; employment, 71; farm workers, 22; importance, 92; media, 38; religion, 70; social interaction, 83–85; urban anthropology, 5, 6; use or misuse, 3

fieldwork, 2, 11, 13, 16, 173, 174

food: access in town, 149; borrow, 135, 136; change in food preparation, 140; consumption categories, 138, 139; Cuca shop, 54; food as wages, 26; food cost, 36, 120, 121, 131, 138; food purchase, 40, 78, 154; household food security, 20; household problem, 140; HSL, 15; informal sector selling, 70, 72; making last, 135, 136; markets, 59; marriage, 122, 126; purchase, 21; solid food, 77; street children, 77

German, 1, 2, 4, 18, 22–26, 28, 38, 42, 51, 61, 71, 96–100, 104, 105, 112, 136, 149, 174

health, 6, 10, 20, 28, 43, 57, 59, 73, 76, 79, 80, 87, 103, 120, 140, 149, 178, 179

Herero: Advisory Board, 28, 43, 44; areas in Katutura, 55, 160; association, 86, 87; cattle, 21; church, 70; communal area, 150, 151; conjugal unions and marriage, 124, 125; cultural traditions, 21, 42, 94; demonstration and shootings in Old Location, 29, 57; description, 93, 94; employment, 71; ethnic group section, 49; ethnic group term, 3; female-centered, 161; in Main Location, 26, 27; in Windhoek, 26; Katutura, 68, 69; Katutura and Old Location rift, 38; language, 90, 96, 97; lineages, 123; loss of cattle, 26; Matutura, 4; name for Windhoek, 24; occupied Windhoek area, 24; population size, 25; schools, 51; stereotypes, 95, 96, 98; talking to, 11; wars, 24; women, 12

household, 137–143, 158–166, 173–175, 177–180; budget, 15; choice on KAT1991, 10; comparisons, 13, 83; composition in communal areas, 18; defined, 110; diversity, 2; dwelling site and dwellings, 110, 111, 113; Eastern Communal Area, 21; economics, 133–138; ethnic homogeneity, 49; features, 111, 112; female-centered household, 10, 114–116, 130–135,

137–140,161–164, 166; headed by one person, 130, 131; income, 72, 74, 83; Kavango, 20; Kunene, 21; median monthly income, 14; male-centered household, 10, 72, 92, 113–116, 130–135, 137–140, 161–164, 166; police raids, 49; problems, 139, 140; quality of housing, 23; resources, 139, 140; size, 132; Southern Communal Area, 22; stayers and returnees, 82; television, 121; types of households, 14, 114–116

Household Subsistence Level (HSL), 14, 15, 137, 164, 166

housing: Advisory Board, 44; Cape Town, 168; characteristics, 54, 55, 59, 113, 163, 168; contract, 48; costs, 113, 135; development, 53, 54, 113, 169; environment, 113, 114, 162; ethnicity, 50; funding, 42; increased cost, 29, 36, 167; influence, 6; Main Location, 29; marriage, 122, 123, 128, 129; migrant labor compound, 38; migration, 152; Municipality, 74; Office, 47; old and new Katutura, 159, 160; privately-owned, 113, 165, 166; problems, 121, 140; quality, 23, 46, 89, 112, 158, 163; records, 12; rental, 113, 150; self built, 27; single quarters, 113; Survey, 50, 175, 177; urbanization, 149

HSL, 14, 15, 137, 164, 166

income: alcohol consumption, 76; beer, 139; child nutrition, 76; female-centered, 131, 133, 135, 136, 160–162; food, 139; household income, 133–135, 137, 138; Household Median, 14; HSL inadequate, 15; Katutura, 42, 83; laborer, 36; low income, 169; median monthly, 72, 159–163; old and new Katutura, 13, 160–161; problems, 141; renting rooms, 27; returnee/stayer, 82; sale of cattle, 151; stereotypes, 98

56, 155; Owambo, 119; sports, 87; status 89–90; street children, 77, 78; teachers, 133

shebeen, 62, 73–75, 85, 86, 89, 90, 133, 149

single quarters, 51, 53, 57, 68, 111, 113, 153, 154, 156

South Africa: Afrikaans, 69; apartheid, 13, 30, 38, 40, 48, 149, 157, 168; beer hall, 73; Broadcasting Corporation, 38; Defense Force, 18, 82; export to, 23; fieldwork, 11; government, 29, 38, 42, 43, 46; HSL, 15; independence from, 2, 14; migration, 168; occupation, 18; people from, 28; police, 47; resentment of, 11; South West Africa and, 1, 26; universities, 52; urban research, 7, 91

squatter, 23, 53, 54, 68, 112, 168

stayer, 31, 61, 82, 162, 163, 180

stereotypes, 67, 71, 84, 95, 98, 103, 167

stratification, 2, 6, 89, 157–159, 161, 162, 165, 166

street children, 77, 103, 167

SWAPO, 31, 54, 61, 71, 82

urbanization, 2, 6, 69, 77, 128, 148, 149, 153, 156, 166, 167, 169

white: Africans, 3, 89; Afrikaans, 97; apartheid, 42, 46; description, 91, 93, 95; drinking, 75, 76; employers and employment, 58, 71, 154; interaction, 99–101; Katutura, 49; living apart, 26; locations, 33; marriage, 121; marriage to blacks, 38, 157; media, 38; proximity to blacks, 29; school, 52; steroetypes, 99, 100, 155; suspicion, 11, 13; taken over land, 26; Windhoek, 40

Zambia, 7, 20, 82

DR. WADE C. PENDLETON, currently Professor of Anthropology at the San Diego State University in California, published his first book on Katutura in 1974. In 1987, after having been refused entry to Namibia for eleven years, he returned to the country to work on well over twenty-five applied social science projects, and many of the findings are contained in his latest book, a discussion of Katutura under and after apartheid.

Monographs in International Studies

Titles Available from Ohio University Press, 1996

Southeast Asia Series

No. 56   **Duiker, William J.** Vietnam Since the Fall of Saigon. 1989. Updated ed. 401 pp. Paper 0-89680-162-4 $20.00.

No. 64   **Dardjowidjojo, Soenjono.** Vocabulary Building in Indonesian: An Advanced Reader. 1984. 664 pp. Paper 0-89680-118-7 $30.00.

No. 65   **Errington, J. Joseph.** Language and Social Change in Java: Linguistic Reflexes of Modernization in a Traditional Royal Polity. 1985. 210 pp. Paper 0-89680-120-9 $25.00.

No. 66   **Binh, Tran Tu.** The Red Earth: A Vietnamese Memoir of Life on a Colonial Rubber Plantation. Tr. by John Spragens. 1984. 102 pp. (SEAT*, V. 5) Paper 0-89680-119-5 $11.00.

No. 68   **Syukri, Ibrahim.** History of the Malay Kingdom of Patani. 1985. 135 pp. Paper 0-89680-123-3 $15.00.

No. 69   **Keeler, Ward.** Javanese: A Cultural Approach. 1984. 559 pp. Paper 0-89680-121-7 $25.00.

No. 70   **Wilson, Constance M. and Lucien M. Hanks.** Burma-Thailand Frontier Over Sixteen Decades: Three Descriptive Documents. 1985. 128 pp. Paper 0-89680-124-1 $11.00.

No. 71   **Thomas, Lynn L. and Franz von Benda-Beckmann,** eds. Change and Continuity in Minangkabau: Local, Regional, and Historical Perspectives on West Sumatra. 1985. 353 pp. Paper 0-89680-127-6 $16.00.

No. 72   **Reid, Anthony and Oki Akira,** eds. The Japanese Experience in Indonesia: Selected Memoirs of 1942–1945. 1986. 424 pp., 20 illus. (SEAT, V. 6) Paper 0-89680-132-2 $20.00.

* Southeast Asia Translation Project Group

No. 74 McArthur M. S. H. Report on Brunei in 1904. Introduced and Annotated by A. V. M. Horton. 1987. 297 pp. Paper 0-89680-135-7 $15.00.

No. 75 Lockard, Craig A. From Kampung to City: A Social History of Kuching, Malaysia, 1820–1970. 1987. 325 pp. Paper 0-89680-136-5 $20.00.

No. 76 McGinn, Richard, ed. Studies in Austronesian Linguistics. 1986. 516 pp. Paper 0-89680-137-3 $20.00.

No. 77 Muego, Benjamin N. Spectator Society: The Philippines Under Martial Rule. 1986. 232 pp. Paper 0-89680-138-1 $17.00.

No 79 Walton, Susan Pratt. Mode in Javanese Music. 1987. 278 pp. Paper 0-89680-144-6 $15.00.

No. 80 Nguyen Anh Tuan. South Vietnam: Trial and Experience. 1987. 477 pp., tables. Paper 0-89680-141-1 $18.00.

No. 82 Spores, John C. Running Amok: An Historical Inquiry. 1988. 190 pp. paper 0-89680-140-3 $13.00.

No. 83 Malaka, Tan. From Jail to Jail. Tr. by Helen Jarvis. 1911. 1209 pp., three volumes. (SEAT V. 8) Paper 0-89680-150-0 $55.00.

No. 84 Devas, Nick, with Brian Binder, Anne Booth, Kenneth Davey, and Roy Kelly. Financing Local Government in Indonesia. 1989. 360 pp. Paper 0-89680-153-5 $20.00.

No. 85 Suryadinata, Leo. Military Ascendancy and Political Culture: A Study of Indonesia's Golkar. 1989. 235 pp., illus., glossary, append., index, bibliog. Paper 0-89680-154-3 $18.00.

No. 86 Williams, Michael. Communism, Religion, and Revolt in Banten in the Early Twentieth Century. 1990. 390 pp. Paper 0-89680-155-1 $14.00.

No. 87 Hudak, Thomas. The Indigenization of Pali Meters in Thai Poetry. 1990. 247 pp. Paper 0-89680-159-4 $15.00.

No. 88 Lay, Ma Ma. Not Out of Hate: A Novel of Burma. Tr. by Margaret Aung-Thwin. Ed. by William Frederick. 1991. 260 pp. (SEAT V. 9) Paper 0-89680-167-5 $20.00.

No. 89 Anwar, Chairil. The Voice of the Night: Complete Poetry and Prose of Chairil Anwar. 1992. Revised Edition. Tr. by Burton Raffel. 196 pp. Paper 0-89680-170-5 $20.00.

No. 90 Hudak, Thomas John, tr., The Tale of Prince Samuttakote: A Buddhist Epic from Thailand. 1993. 230 pp. Paper 0-89680-174-8 $20.00.

No. 91 Roskies, D. M., ed. Text/Politics in Island Southeast Asia: Essays in Interpretation. 1993. 330 pp. Paper 0-89680-175-6 $25.00.

No. 92 Schenkhuizen, Marguérite, translated by Lizelot Stout van Balgooy. Memoirs of an Indo Woman: Twentieth-Century Life in the East Indies and Abroad. 1993. 312 pp. Paper 0-89680-178-0 $25.00.

No. 93   **Salleh, Muhammad Haji.** Beyond the Archipelago: Selected Poems. 1995. 247 pp. Paper 0-89680-181-0 $20.00.

No. 94   **Federspiel, Howard M.** A Dictionary of Indonesian Islam. 1995. 327 pp. Bibliog. Paper 0-89680-182-9 $25.00.

No. 95   **Leary, John.** Violence and the Dream People: The Orang Asli in the Malayan Emergency 1948–1960. 1995. 275 pp. Maps, illus., tables, appendices, bibliog., index. Paper 0-89680-186-1 $22.00.

No. 96   **Lewis, Dianne.** *Jan Compagnie* in the Straits of Malacca 1641–1795. 1995. 176 pp. Map, appendices, bibliog., index. Paper 0-89680-187-x. $18.00.

Africa Series

No. 43   **Harik, Elsa M. and Donald G. Schilling.** The Politics of Education in Colonial Algeria and Kenya. 1984. 102 pp. Paper 0-89680-117-9 $12.50.

No. 45   **Keto, C. Tsehloane.** American-South African Relations 1784–1980: Review and Select Bibliography. 1985. 169 pp. Paper 0-89680-128-4 $11.00.

No. 46   **Burness, Don,** ed. Wanasema: Conversations with African Writers. 1985. 103 pp. paper 0-89680-129-2 $11.00.

No. 47   **Switzer, Les.** Media and Dependency in South Africa: A Case Study of the Press and the Ciskei "Homeland." 1985. 97 pp. Paper 0-89680-130-6 $10.00.

No. 49   **Hart, Ursula Kingsmill.** Two Ladies of Colonial Algeria: The Lives and Times of Aurelie Picard and Isabelle Eberhardt. 1987. 153 pp. paper 0-89680-143-8 $11.00.

No. 51   **Clayton, Anthony and David Killingray.** Khaki and Blue: Military and Police in British Colonial Africa. 1989. 347 pp. Paper 0-89680-147-0 $20.00.

No. 52   **Northrup, David.** Beyond the Bend in the River: African Labor in Eastern Zaire, 1865–1940. 1988. 282 pp. Paper 0-89680-151-9 $15.00.

No. 53   **Makinde, M. Akin.** African Philosophy, Culture, and Traditional Medicine. 1988. 172 pp. Paper 0-89680-152-7 $16.00.

No. 54   **Parson, Jack,** ed. Succession to High Office in Botswana: Three Case Studies. 1990. 455 pp. Paper 0-89680-157-8 $20.00.

No. 56   **Staudinger, Paul.** In the Heart of the Hausa States. Tr. by Johanna E. Moody. Foreword by Paul Lovejoy. 1990. In two volumes., 469 + 224 pp., maps, apps. Paper 0-89680-160-8 (2 vols.) $35.00.

No. 57   **Sikainga, Ahmad Alawad.** The Western Bahr Al-Ghazal under British Rule, 1898–1956. 1991. 195 pp. Paper 0-89680-161-6 $15.00.

No. 58   Wilson, Louis E. The Krobo People of Ghana to 1892: A Political and Social History. 1991. 285 pp. Paper 0-89680-164-0 $20.00.

No. 59   du Toit, Brian M. Cannabis, Alcohol, and the South African Student: Adolescent Drug Use, 1974–1985. 1991. 176 pp., notes, tables. Paper 0-89680-166-7 $17.00.

No. 60   Falola, Toyin and Dennis Itavyar, eds. The Political Economy of Health in Africa. 1992. 258 pp., notes, tables. Paper 0-89680-166-7 $20.00.

No. 61   Kiros, Tedros. Moral Philosophy and Development: The Human Condition in Africa. 1992. 199 pp., notes. Paper 0-89680-171-3 $20.00.

No. 62   Burness, Don. Echoes of the Sunbird: An Anthology of Contemporary African Poetry. 1993. 198 pp. Paper 0-89680-173-x $17.00.

No. 63   Glew, Robert S. and Chaibou Babalé. Hausa Folktales from Niger. 1993. 143 pp. Paper 0-89680-176-4 $15.00.

No. 64   Nelson, Samuel H. Colonialism in the Congo Basin 1880–1940. 1994. 290 pp. Index. Paper 0-89680-180-2 $23.00.

Latin America Series

No. 9   Tata, Robert J. Structural Changes in Puerto Rico's Economy: 1947–1976. 1981. 118 pp. paper 0-89680-107-1 $12.00.

No. 12   Wallace, Brian F. Ownership and Development: A Comparison of Domestic and Foreign Firms in Colombian Manufacturing. 1987. 185 pp. Paper 0-89680-145-4 $10.00.

No. 13   Henderson, James D. Conservative Thought in Latin America: The Ideas of Laureano Gomez. 1988. 229 pp. Paper 0-89680-148-9 $16.00.

No. 16   Alexander, Robert J. Juscelino Kubitschek and the Development of Brazil. 1991. 500 pp., notes, bibliog. Paper 0-89680-163-2 $33.00.

No. 17   Mijeski, Kenneth J., ed. The Nicaraguan Constitution of 1987: English Translation and Commentary. 1991. 355 pp. Paper 0-89680-165-9 $25.00.

No. 18   Finnegan, Pamela. The Tension of Paradox: José Donoso's *The Obscene Bird of Night* as Spiritual Exercises. 1992. 204 pp. Paper 0-89680-169-1 $15.00.

No. 19   Kim, Sung Ho and Thomas W. Walker, eds. Perspectives on War and Peace in Central America. 1992. 155 pp., notes, bibliog. Paper 0-89680-172-1 $17.00.

No. 20   Becker, Marc. Mariátegui and Latin American Marxist Theory. 1993. 239 pp. Paper 0-89680-177-2 $20.00.

No. 21   Boschetto-Sandoval, Sandra M. and Marcia Phillips McGowan, eds.

Claribel Alegría and Central American Literature. 1994. 233 pp., illus. Paper 0-89680-179-9 $20.00.

No. 22 **Zimmerman, Marc.** Literature and Resistance in Guatemala: Textual Modes and Cultural Politics from El Señor Presidente to Rigoberta Menchú. 1995. 2 volume set 320 + 370 pp., notes, bibliog. Paper 0-89680-183-7 $50.00.

No. 23 **Hey, Jeanne A. K.** Theories of Dependent Foreign Policy: The Case of Ecuador in the 1980s. 1995. 280 pp., map, tables, notes, bibliog., index. paper 0-89680-184-5 $22.00.

No. 24 **Wright, Bruce E.** Theory in the Practice of the Nicaraguan Revolution. 1995. 320 pp., notes, illus., bibliog., index. Paper 0-89680-185-3. $23.00.

Ordering Information

Individuals are encouraged to patronize local bookstores wherever possible. Orders for titles in the Monographs in International Studies may be placed directly through the Ohio University Press, Scott Quadrangle, Athens, Ohio 45701-2979. Individuals should remit payment by check, VISA, or MasterCard.* Those ordering from the United Kingdom, Continental Europe, the Middle East,. and Africa should order through Academic and University Publishers Group, 1 Gower Street, London WC1E, England. Orders from the Pacific Region, Asia, Australia, and New Zealand should be sent to East-West Export Books, c/o the University of Hawaii Press, 2840 Kolowalu Street, Honolulu, Hawaii 96822, USA.

Individuals ordering from outside of the U.S. should remit in U.S. funds to Ohio University Press either by International Money Order or by a check drawn on a U.S. bank.** Most out-of-print titles may be ordered from University Microfilms, Inc., 300 North Zeeb Road, Ann Arbor, Michigan 48106, USA.

Prices are subject to change.

---

* Please add $3.50 for the first book and $.75 for each additional book for shipping and handling.

** Outside the U.S. please add $4.50 for the first book and $.75 for each additional book.

Ohio University
Monographs in International Studies

The Ohio University Center for International Studies was established to help create within the university and local communities a greater awareness of the world beyond the United States. Comprising programs in African, Latin American, Southeast Asian, Development and Administrative studies, the Center supports scholarly research, sponsors lectures and colloquia, encourages course development within the university curriculum, and publishes the Monographs in International Studies series with the Ohio University Press. The Center and its programs also offer an interdisciplinary Master of Arts degree in which students may focus on one of the regional or topical concentrations, and may also combine academics with training in career fields such as journalism, business, and language teaching. For undergraduates, major and certificate programs are also available.

For more information, contact the Vice Provost for International Studies, Burson House, Ohio University, Athens, Ohio 45701.